TASTE the SEASONS

Woodside-Atherton Auxiliary to Children's Hospital at Stanford

Editor
LINDA BRANDT

Art Director
ANN REMEN-WILLIS

Photographer
NIKOLAY ŽUREK

Typographer
JONATHAN PECK TYPOGRAPHERS, LTD.

Lithographer
NORTHWESTERN COLORGRAPHICS
PRODUCTION RESOURCE

Printer
KINGSPORT PRESS

Library of Congress Catalog Card Number: 85-51259

ISBN 0-9615260-0-9

Acknowledgment

This book could not have been realized without the enthusiasm and cooperation of the Woodside-Atherton Auxiliary membership and the Allied Arts Guild staff, without the encouragement of the Auxiliary Board of Directors for 1983 through 1985, without the many women whose countless hours were spent contributing and testing recipes, without the generous support of families, friends, and townspeople, without the creative expertise, wisdom, and patience of the professionals who gave so generously of themselves, and most of all, without our love and belief in children.

Cookbook Committee

Food Editor
DONNA HICKS

Project Director
TITA KOLOZSI

JUDY ADAMS	JEANNE LARKIN	ELIE SKINNER
MARJ BERLIN	BETTY NAYLOR	CHRIS STEIN
LIZ BROWNELL	JACKIE SCANDALIOS	CAROL WILLIAMS

Arcata Graphics Company has generously underwritten the cost of printing **TASTE the SEASONS**. The Woodside-Atherton Auxiliary gratefully acknowledges this kind gift and thanks the staff of Arcata Graphics Company for its valuable advice and support.

CONTENTS

Spring

Summer

Autumn

Winter

INTRODUCTION

California, perhaps more than any other of our fifty states, has become a meeting place for people from all over the world. Beginning with the Spanish explorers and continuing through 135 years of statehood, California has welcomed people from every nation and every state in the Union. In the past 30 years, attractive career opportunities and a moderate climate have encouraged a new wave of settlers to make California their home. The traditions and cultures of these new Californians have blended and mixed together with the old to produce a unique way of life.

TASTE the SEASONS is a collection of seasonal recipes and entertaining ideas that reflect the California way of life. Like California itself, this book is a combination of many influences—old and new, foreign and regional, traditional and experimental. An eagerness to blend these influences and a mild climate yielding an enormous bounty of fresh fruit and vegetables have encouraged Californians to create and present a wonderful assortment of dishes with the freshest of ingredients.

Even though the changes in climate are more subtle in California than in other states, the fruit, vegetables, and flowers grown here vary with each season. We have tried to reflect the seasonal changes, however subtle, in our

recipes and in our suggestions for entertaining.

TASTE the SEASONS is written for the person who finds enjoyment in serving attractive, delicious meals to family and friends alike. Most of the recipes in the book have been selected for either occasion. Some of the more traditional ones such as Cobb Salad and Persimmon Pudding with Lemon Sauce, offer a hearty, guaranteed-to-please flavor that has been treasured and passed down over the years through generations of good cooks.

Other recipes like fresh Artichoke Soup, Grilled Halibut with Cucumbers, and Strawberry Sorbet with Grand Marnier, reflect a trend toward lighter fare. Most recipes don't require long hours in the kitchen. Some can be prepared, either completely or in part, well in advance. In many instances, you'll find our suggestions for serving California wines as well as ideas for accompaniments and side dishes.

More than 40 color pictures, inspired by and photographed throughout the grounds of Allied Arts Guild, offer diversity in presentation that we hope will encourage you to experiment and add your own personal touch when entertaining.

Recipes calling for luscious strawberries, fragrant pears, and the flavor of apricots find their way into first

courses and desserts. You'll find avocados and artichokes, leeks and red peppers, cracked crab, Pacific seafood, and spring lamb—all suggested and presented according to season. And what cookbook from California would be complete without the addition of at least one luscious chocolate dessert?

Whether you dine indoors or out, in a country kitchen or formal dining room, the addition of decorative touches, whether small or on the grandest scale, add a special touch.

You can begin a table setting, regardless of the season, by choosing favorite items from a personal collection. An heirloom embroidered cloth or old quilt, a prized antique basket, or small items collected during a recent trip, make ideal choices for creating an interesting table.

Flowers add to the festive spirit of almost any occasion and can express a seasonal mood. Casual garden bouquets seem to echo the lazy, relaxed feeling of summer. A mixture of dried leaves and pods brightened with fresh or silk flowers reflect the crisp feel and colors of autumn. A combination of evergreens and foliages with cinnamon candy sticks add spark to the excitement of winter holidays. And flowering bulbs, such as crocus, hyacinth, and narcissus, signal the beginning of spring.

Try the seasonal approach when choosing accessories and decorations, too. A jovial scarecrow and bales of hay enhance the harvest theme for a fall tailgate party. Flags, streamers, and straw hats salute the Fourth of July. Topiary animals add a touch of whimsy to any garden table. And lacy white linens bring the fresh look of spring to a formal dinner party. Whatever the event, let the ideas in **TASTE the SEASONS** inspire you to add fun and delight to your next party.

Most of the photographs in **TASTE the SEASONS** were taken at Allied Arts Guild in Menlo Park, California. Originally a piece of the vast Rancho de las Pulgas, a land grant from the King of Spain, the property was purchased in 1929 by Mr. and Mrs. Garfield Merner as a site for a crafts guild. Today, nearby residents and visitors continue to enjoy the lovely gardens, tea room, and charming shops.

The Woodside-Atherton Auxiliary, publisher of **TASTE the SEASONS**, staffs the Traditional Shop and administers Allied Arts Guild for the benefit of Children's Hospital at Stanford. All proceeds from the sale of **TASTE the SEASONS** will be donated to Children's Hospital where patient care and research today will lead to healthier and happier lives for children tomorrow.

PHOTOGRAPHS

Spring

Pages 10 and 11

Old wooden trellis supports 40-year-old wisteria blooming near the Barn at the Guild.

Japanese cherry blossoms form a lacy curtain outside Traditional Shop window.

An afternoon dessert party is set beneath a canopy of lavender wisteria. Brightly-wrapped packages suggest color scheme and topiary goose adds whimsy as centerpiece. Lovely English silver samovar and Haviland dessert plates complete elegant theme.

Hand-painted wooden eggs pair with striking bouquet of colorful spring tulips.

Pink Marguerites brighten pathways of Guild throughout April and May.

Pages 30 and 31

Napkin-lined basket laden with seasonal melon, luscious strawberries, and Morning Glory Muffins greet early risers.

Epitome of freshness—grilled halibut with sautéed cucumbers, miniature carrots, and savory rice. China by Chloe.

Embroidered Chinese grass linen cloth, doilies lining white Imperatrice china, and centerpiece of white spring flowers accented by trailing clematis illustrate lacy, all-white theme for elegant dinner party.

Summer

Pages 42 and 43

Warm California sunshine greets visitors to Allied Arts patio where blue wrought iron furniture has become a trademark.

Handmade, terra cotta roof tiles, typical of colonial Spanish architecture, shelter a courtyard.

Guests are expected in the Court of Abundance amid spectacular display of annuals and perennials.

Molly, the Guild's resident feline, enjoys afternoon nap on one of many handcarved wooden benches located throughout gardens.

Antique tole coffee urn from France displays graceful arrangement of wax flowers and delphiniums of varying hues.

Pages 62 and 63

Niçoise pasta salad composed on glass salad plate.

Delicate flavor of chilled minted pea soup is served in Luneville French soup bowl from Traditional Shop.

Single alstremeria, tucked into beribboned napkin, mirrors colors of Chantilly plate by Fitz & Floyd.

Refreshing temptation for summer—strawberry sorbet in frosty stemware accompanied by toffee almond cookies.

Autumn

Winter

Visitors to the courtyard take special note of fresco mural by Pedro de Lemos.

Archways, thick plaster walls, and decorative wrought iron are typical of colonial Spanish architecture.

Antiques set the mood for glorious wine-tasting picnic outside the Barn, an original ranchero building from the early 1800's. Old wine press centerpiece rests on Killim rug.

Happy face of carved pumpkin perches on stairs near Guild's main entrance.

Autumn produces untold wealth of dried materials that handsomely combine with fresh cut flowers. Bittersweet, dried oak leaves, and Red Rover mums are arranged in antique basket.

Fresh shellfish—scallops, mussels, and jumbo shrimp—enhance herb and tomato-laced pasta.

Persimmons grow in abundance on courtyard trees at Guild. Steamed pudding, baked in a decorative mold, makes an ideal holiday gift.

Unusual objects from a private collection add visual interest to serene Oriental setting. Antique Chinese wedding basket, cinnabar and tortoise shell boxes, and porcelain roosters compliment Imari plates.

Valencia oranges lend color to the Guild's winter landscape.

Aged port, served in Waterford cordial glasses, rests on antique silver tray. Single branch of flowering quince foretells Spring.

Fresh Dungeness crab, crusty sourdough bread, salad of mixed greens, and chilled wine transform fireplace corner into cozy dining area for two.

A visit to the beautifully decorated tree at Allied Arts is a holiday tradition.

Let elegant accessories create mood for intimate New Year's celebration. Candle in antique tole inkwell shines on glittered mask invitation set near opera glasses and colorful confetti. Who could resist grilled oysters and champagne served at the stroke of midnight?

Roasted holiday goose, trimmed with sautéed apples and red currant cabbage, and Brussels sprouts flecked with mustard seeds, are presented on pewter serving platter.

Tangy Dijon-style vinaigrette enhances subtle flavor of braised leeks in this delicious first-course recipe.

SPRING

Clockwise from top: Spring arrives with displays of colorful tulips and pink Marguerites; dessert sampling of Chocolate Mousse Torte (page 40), Lemon Macaroon Torte (page 36), Fruit Tarts (page 71), and Strawberry Cream Cake (page 38); Traditional Shop glassware; April-blooming wisteria.

Camembert Mousse

1   envelope unflavored
    gelatin

¼   cup warm water

2   to 3 ounces
    Camembert cheese,
    rind removed

4   ounces blue cheese

1   teaspoon
    Worcestershire

1   egg, separated

½   cup heavy cream

    Rye crackers or sliced
    baguette

    Watercress sprigs

Lightly oil the inside of a decorative 2½-cup mold; set aside.

Sprinkle gelatin over warm water and set aside for 5 minutes to dissolve.

Place Camembert and blue cheese in blender or food processor along with Worcestershire, egg yolk, and gelatin. Whirl until smooth.

In separate bowls, whip egg white and heavy cream until stiff peaks form. Transfer cheese mixture into a large bowl and fold in whipped egg white, then whipped cream, just until combined. Spoon into prepared mold; cover, and refrigerate for at least 8 hours or overnight.

To serve, lower mold part-way into a shallow pan of lukewarm water—just a few seconds or long enough to loosen sides. Shake mold once or twice, testing to be sure mousse is free. Invert onto serving plate and encircle with crackers or slices of baguette. Garnish with watercress sprigs.

Makes 12 servings

Marinated Scallops in Red Pepper Purée

Set peppers in a shallow roasting pan and place 2 to 3 inches from broiler element. Broil, turning frequently with tongs, until peppers are well blistered and appear charred on all sides. Transfer to a brown paper bag. Close bag tightly and set aside for 15 to 20 minutes, allowing peppers to sweat and loosen their skins. Cool and then peel off skins; cut peppers in half, remove seeds, and place in food processor.

Whirl peppers until smooth; then add vinegar, oil, and salt and pepper to taste. Cover and refrigerate. (Or, refrigerate up to 2 days, if made ahead.)

Slice scallops in half and place in a small bowl. Pour over lime juice and marinate for 2 to 4 hours or until they turn opaque.

Just before serving, peel avocados and cut into thin slices. Place a pool of purée on each plate. Arrange a few slices of avocado to one side. Using a slotted spoon, lift out scallops, draining briefly, and place attractively on top of purée. Garnish with watercress.

Makes 6 servings

4	large red peppers
2½	tablespoons raspberry vinegar
2	tablespoons extra virgin olive oil
	Salt and pepper to taste
1	pound large scallops
1	cup fresh lime juice (or lemon juice)
2	avocados
	Watercress sprigs

You may substitute a 7½-ounce jar of roasted peppers for the fresh, if you prefer, but we feel the flavor and appearance of such a substitution detracts from the freshness of this unusual first course. Serve with a glass of Sauvignon Blanc as pictured on page 31.

Prosciutto-wrapped Asparagus

Crème Fraîche

½   *cup heavy cream*

2   *tablespoons sour cream*

¼   *cup crème fraîche (see directions at right)*

1¼   *teaspoons Dijon mustard*

18   *to 20 medium-size asparagus*

4   *to 5 large slices prosciutto*

     Herbs de Provence

To make crème fraîche, combine cream and sour cream in a small bowl. Cover loosely with plastic wrap and set aside at room temperature for 24 hours.

Measure ¼ cup crème fraîche and combine with mustard (reserve remaining crème frâiche for other uses).

Trim asparagus to 5 inches long and peel stems. Steam over boiling water for about 5 minutes until tender crisp. Plunge into cold water to stop the cooking process, then drain well on paper towels.

Cut slices of prosciutto in half lengthwise, then cut each in half crosswise. You should have 4 strips of prosciutto from each slice.

Spread a little mustard on one piece of prosciutto. Sprinkle with herbs and position an asparagus spear on top. Roll up so that tips of asparagus are exposed at both ends. Repeat with remaining ingredients.

Arrange 3 spears on each salad plate. Offer as a first course, either slightly chilled or at room temperature.

Makes about 6 servings

Suggested accompaniments to follow this delicious first course include Salmon in Puff Pastry (page 22) served with steamed seasonal vegetables. By trimming the length of the asparagus to 3 inches, you can serve Prosciutto-wrapped Asparagus as an hors d'oeuvre. Arrange them on a serving platter in a spoke fashion with tips pointing inward.

Artichoke Soup

Trim off top of each artichoke. Peel off outer leaves and trim bottom stem. Place in a large pot with enough water to cover. Add lemon juice, garlic, and salt. Bring to a boil and cook, uncovered, for 30 to 40 minutes until tender. Drain and cool completely.

Remove leaves and scrape tender pulp from each one directly into a measuring cup. Remove and discard yellow and purple inner leaves; remove the fuzzy choke from the inside of each artichoke. Cut up artichoke bottom and add to the pulp. (You should have a total of about 2 cups.)

Combine artichoke pulp, chicken stock, and lemon juice in a medium saucepan. Simmer, uncovered, for about 10 minutes.

Meanwhile, melt butter in a frying pan over medium heat. Add shallots and garlic and sauté for 1 minute. Add flour and cook for 1 minute until bubbly. Slowly whisk in about 1 cup artichoke stock, stirring until combined. Return mixture to the saucepan and stir until blended.

Whirl soup (in batches, if necessary) in a blender or food processor until smooth. Add sherry and season to taste with salt and pepper. (At this point, you may cover and refrigerate up to 8 hours or overnight.)

To serve, bring soup to a simmer over low heat. Add cream and heat to serving temperature.

Makes 4 servings

3   *large artichokes*

Cooking Liquid

2   *tablespoons lemon juice*

2   *or 3 cloves garlic, chopped*

1   *teaspoon salt*

2   *cups chicken stock*

2   *teaspoons lemon juice*

2   *tablespoons butter*

1   *tablespoon minced shallots*

1   *small clove garlic, minced*

2   *tablespoons all-purpose flour*

1   *tablespoon dry sherry*

¼   *teaspoon salt*

    Freshly ground pepper

⅔   *to 1 cup half-and-half*

Fresh Artichokes Vinaigrette

2 tablespoons lemon juice

1 quart cold water

16 small artichokes (about 3 inches in diameter)

Dressing

¼ cup tarragon vinegar

1 teaspoon salt

½ teaspoon freshly ground pepper

1 tablespoon Dijon mustard

1 egg yolk

¾ cup olive oil

½ pound mushrooms

Red leaf lettuce

Cherry tomatoes, halved

Watercress

Combine lemon juice and cold water in a large bowl. Trim off top of each artichoke. Peel off all the tough outer leaves down past the pale green inner ones. (It's important to remove them completely otherwise the artichokes will remain tough, even after cooking.) Peel the stem, too. As each artichoke is finished, drop it into the acid water to prevent discoloration.

Drain artichokes, rinse under running water, and transfer to a large pot. Add enough boiling water to cover and cook over medium high heat for 8 to 10 minutes or until artichokes can be pierced easily with a fork. (Taste a leaf or two—if they still are tough, return artichokes to heat and cook longer.)

Meanwhile, whisk together vinegar, salt, pepper, mustard, and egg yolk in a small bowl. Slowly add olive oil, whisking until blended.

Drain artichokes well. Cool, then cut into quarters; place in a bowl and spoon over half the dressing. Toss to combine; cover, and refrigerate until chilled. Slice mushrooms, wrap in plastic, and refrigerate until chilled.

Combine artichokes, mushrooms, and remaining dressing. Arrange a few lettuce leaves on each salad plate and place a small mound of salad on top. Garnish edges of plate with cherry tomatoes and watercress.

Makes 6 to 8 servings

Prawns Vinaigrette with Snow Peas & Mushrooms

Whisk together mustard, lime juice, and dill in a small bowl. Add oils slowly, whisking to combine. Season to taste with salt and pepper.

Blanch prawns in gently simmering water for 2 to 3 minutes or until just pink. Cool to room temperature, then refrigerate until cold.

When prawns are very cold, peel and devein, leaving the tails attached to 8 of the largest ones. Cut these prawns in half lengthwise, just to—but not through—the tails. (These will be used for garnish.) Slice remaining prawns in fourths and set aside.

Blanch snow peas in boiling salted water for 1 or 2 minutes. Plunge into cold water to stop cooking; drain and slice diagonally into 3 pieces. Spread pine nuts in a dry frying pan and place over medium heat, shaking pan continuously, until lightly toasted.

Combine prawn pieces, snowpeas, nuts, onion, and mushrooms in a bowl. Pour over some of the vinaigrette and toss gently.

Place a leaf of lettuce on each salad plate. Mound a spoonful of salad on each leaf, arranging 1 reserved prawn to one side in such a way that the tail stands upright. Serve immediately and offer remaining vinaigrette separately.

Makes 8 servings

Vinaigrette

2	tablespoons Dijon mustard
¼	cup fresh lime juice (2 limes)
1½	tablespoons minced fresh dill
½	cup olive oil
½	cup vegetable oil
	Salt and freshly ground pepper
20	large prawns (about 1½ lbs.)
½	pound snow peas, trimmed
¼	to ⅓ cup pine nuts
3	tablespoons finely minced red onion
½	pound mushrooms, thinly sliced
8	large leaves butter lettuce

Serve this first course with Chardonnay followed by Veal Noisettes in Basil Cream (page 27) and Lemon Macaroon Torte (page 36).

Spinach Salad with Pancetta

2   small bunches fresh
    spinach (about 1¼
    lbs.), torn in pieces

½   pound Italian
    pancetta (cut
    ¼-inch-thick), cut
    into pieces

3   tablespoons olive oil

2   tablespoons vegetable
    oil

½   teaspoon Tabasco

4   green onions
    (including some
    tops), thinly sliced

½   pound mushrooms,
    sliced

2   tablespoons Dijon or
    other wine-grained
    mustard

2   teaspoons lemon juice

2   tablespoons grated
    Parmesan cheese

Remove stems from spinach leaves. Wash, drain well, and blot off excess moisture with paper towels. Place in a large serving bowl.

Cook pancetta in a wide frying pan over medium heat for 4 to 5 minutes until lightly crisp. Remove with a slotted spoon and drain; set aside. Pour off all but 1 tablespoon drippings.

Whisk in olive oil, vegetable oil, and Tabasco, scraping bottom of pan to deglaze. Stir in green onions and cook over low heat for 3 minutes. Stir in mushrooms, mustard, and lemon juice; continue simmering for 2 to 3 minutes longer.

Pour hot dressing over spinach, tossing gently until well coated. Sprinkle with reserved pancetta and grated Parmesan cheese to serve immediately.

Makes 4 to 6 servings

Pancetta—unsmoked Italian bacon—adds flavor to the dressing as well as the salad. It's available at most delicatessens and from shops specializing in Italian foodstuffs. Serve our version of wilted spinach salad with homemade breadsticks or slices of Focaccio (page 66).

Won Ton Chicken Salad

Combine vinegar, sugar, salt, and pepper in a small bowl. Whisk in vegetable and sesame oils. Cover and refrigerate.

Toast sesame seeds in a dry wide frying pan over medium heat, shaking pan frequently, for 3 to 4 minutes until golden. Set aside to cool, then transfer to a small bowl.

Cut won tons into ¼-inch-wide strips. Heat oil in a frying pan. Add won ton pieces, a few at a time, and lightly fry until golden brown. Remove and drain on paper towels.

Combine chicken, onion, pepper, sesame seeds, and lettuce. Pour over half the dressing and toss gently. Just before serving, add won tons and toss gently. Serve immediately and offer remaining dressing separately.

Makes 4 servings

Dressing

⅓	*cup cider vinegar*
4	*teaspoons sugar*
1	*teaspoon salt*
¼	*teaspoon pepper*
⅓	*cup vegetable oil*
⅓	*cup sesame oil*
¼	*cup sesame seeds*
10	*won ton skins*
⅓	*cup vegetable oil*
3	*cups (2 whole breasts), shredded cooked chicken*
4	*green onions (including tops), thinly sliced on diagonal*
1	*medium red pepper, seeded and diced*
4	*cups shredded Romaine lettuce*

Won tons may be fried in advance and then stored in an airtight container until ready to use.

Grilled Halibut with Cucumbers

Herb Butter

6   tablespoons melted
     butter

3   tablespoons minced
     fresh dill

2½   teaspoons lemon
     juice

1   tablespoon minced
     parlsey

½   teaspoon minced
     lemon zest

     Salt and freshly
     ground pepper

6   halibut steaks (each
     about 1 inch thick)

2   English cucumbers,
     peeled and thinly
     sliced

     Salt and freshly
     ground pepper

     Sprigs of dill

Combine melted butter and dill in a measuring cup. Spoon 2 tablespoons into a wide frying pan; set aside. Place remaining herb butter in a small pan along with lemon juice, parsley, lemon zest, and salt and pepper to taste. Place near grill and keep warm.

Wipe fish with a damp cloth. Lightly grease the barbecue grill (or stovetop grill) with oil. Arrange fish on hot grill, positioned 4 to 6 inches above a solid bed of low-glowing coals. Brush each steak generously with melted herb butter. Grill, basting occasionally and turning once to brown both sides, for 8 to 10 minutes (4 to 5 minutes per side). (Or, arrange fish on broiler pan and brush with butter. Broil, 4 to 6 inches below element, for 5 to 8 minutes per side, basting occasionally with additional butter.) Fish should appear flaky near the thickest part when tested with a fork.

Meanwhile, place frying pan over high heat. Add cucumber slices and sauté, stirring often, for 3 to 4 minutes or until tender crisp. Season to taste with salt and pepper.

Arrange fish down the middle of a long serving platter and spoon remaining herb butter over top. Line edges of platter with cucumbers and garnish with sprigs of fresh dill.

Makes 6 servings

Shown in the photograph on page 30 are our suggestions to complete the menu—baby carrots in cognac (page 29), your favorite rice, and a dry crisp Chardonnay. And for dessert, Layered Lemon Pie (page 35).

Tequila Shrimp with Rice

Peel and devein shrimp, leaving tails intact. Place in a small bowl. Cover with lime juice and marinate for 15 to 20 minutes.

Meanwhile, prepare rice and keep warm.

Peel avocado and cut into thick slices, dropping them into a shallow bowl of cold water (to prevent darkening). Drain and set nearby. Heat butter in a very large frying pan over medium heat. Lift shrimp from marinade and sauté, stirring often, for 1 to 2 minutes or just until they begin to turn pink. Remove with a slotted spoon; keep warm. Sauté onion for about 1 minute in reserved pan juices, then carefully pour in tequila (avoid flaming).

Whisk in cream and cook for 1 minute. Season to taste with salt and pepper. Then return shrimp to sauce along with avocado slices, shaking pan gently for a few seconds until heated through. Sprinkle with cilantro.

Serve immediately with hot steamed rice, garnished with sprigs of cilantro and lime slices.

Makes 4 servings

1½	pounds medium-size shrimp
¼	cup (2 to 3 limes) fresh lime juice
	About 4 cups hot steamed rice
1	large avocado
2	tablespoons butter
¼	cup finely chopped green onion
¼	cup tequila
½	cup heavy cream
	Salt and pepper
2	tablespoons finely chopped cilantro
	Sprigs of cilantro
	Thin slices of lime

To add interest to any meal calling for rice, try molding each serving into a fancy shape. Lightly butter four small custard cups— miniature charlotte or brioche molds work well, too—and then press in about 1 cup cooked rice. Serve Tequila Shrimp with a salad of mixed greens, steamed sugar snap peas, and White Zinfandel or Pinot Noir Blanc.

Salmon in Puff Pastry

Poaching Stock

3	cups water
1	cup dry white wine
6	to 8 sprigs parsley
1	small onion, diced
¼	teaspoon dried oregano leaves
8	salmon fillets (about 6 oz. each), skinned
½	cup mayonnaise
1	tablespoon minced fresh dill
2	sheets frozen puff pastry, thawed
1	lightly beaten egg mixed with 1 tablespoon water

Sauce

3	lightly beaten eggs
1	tablespoon Dijon mustard
3	tablespoons lemon juice
1½	cups melted butter
	Sprigs of dill

Combine water, wine, parsley, onion, and oregano in a wide frying pan over low heat. When simmering, add salmon pieces. Cover and poach for 6 to 8 minutes. Remove and cool. Combine mayonnaise and dill in a small bowl.

Roll out each sheet of pastry, one at a time on a floured board, to at least a 12-inch square. Using a straight-edge and sharp knife, trim each sheet to exactly 12 inches square. Then cut both squares in fourths, making eight 6-inch squares.

Brush some egg wash on each pastry square. Trim salmon, if necessary, and center on pastry squares. Top each with 1 tablespoon flavored mayonnaise. Fold up the four corners towards the center—like making an envelope. Pinch (or fold over) edges to seal completely. (At this point, you may cover and chill for up to 6 hours; bring to room temperature before baking.)

Preheat oven to 400°. Lightly grease a rimmed baking sheet with shortening. Brush tops of pastry packages with some egg wash and place on prepared pan. Bake for 20 to 25 minutes or until pastry puffs and is lightly browned.

Meanwhile, whisk eggs, mustard, and lemon juice in the top of a double boiler over simmering water. When warm, slowly begin to add hot melted butter, a few drops at a time, and whisk to incorporate. Continue adding butter in a slow steady stream until thickened. Remove from heat and place in gravy boat.

Arrange a salmon package on each plate. Lay a sprig of dill on top. Offer sauce separately.

Makes 8 servings

Chicken Breasts—Two Methods

Cut each half chicken breast into three long pieces (or fillets). Dip each piece into flour, shaking off the excess. Sprinkle with salt and pepper.

To make garlic-parsley chicken, melt butter and oil in a very wide frying pan over medium-high heat. Sauté, turning pieces over to brown all sides, for 3 to 4 minutes. Sprinkle with garlic and parsley; toss for about 30 seconds (take care not to let garlic brown). Serve immediately.

To make lemon chicken, sauté chicken pieces as directed above. Transfer to an ovenproof dish and keep warm.

Pour off any excess grease from the pan. Add wine and lemon juice, whisking over medium-high heat to deglaze pan. Add parsley and remove from heat. Spoon some sauce over chicken to serve.

Makes 4 to 6 servings

3   *whole chicken breasts, split, boned, and skinned*

   All-purpose flour

   Salt and freshly ground pepper

2   *to 3 tablespoons butter*

1   *tablespoon olive oil*

Garlic-Parsley

2   *or 3 cloves garlic, minced*

1   *to 2 tablespoons chopped parsley*

Lemon

½   *cup dry white wine*

2   *tablespoons lemon juice*

¼   *cup minced parsley*

Here are two quick ways to fix boneless chicken breasts. They are easy-to-prepare, delicious, and perfect when preparation time is at a premium. Our suggested accompaniments include Spinach Salad with Pancetta (page 18), Baby Carrots (page 29), and a bottle of Sauvignon Blanc. For dessert, why not try Fresh Fruit with Ice Cream & Crème Anglaise (page 70)?

Chicken Soufflé Roll

Filling

2	tablespoons butter
4	green onions (including tops), thinly sliced
¼	pound mushrooms, finely chopped
2	packages (1½ cups) frozen chopped spinach, thawed and squeezed of excess moisture
1½	cups shredded cooked chicken
⅓	cup grated sharp Cheddar cheese
1	package (3 oz.) cream cheese, cut in chunks
2	teaspoons Dijon mustard
¼	teaspoon ground nutmeg
	Salt and pepper to taste

To make filling, melt butter in a medium frying pan. Add onions and mushrooms and sauté over medium heat for 2 to 3 minutes until tender. Stir in spinach and cook for 1 minute longer. Add Cheddar cheese, chicken, and cream cheese, cooking just until melted. Stir in mustard, nutmeg, salt, and pepper. Set aside while making soufflé; or cool, cover, and refrigerate, if made ahead.

Preheat oven to 350°. Line bottom of a 10½ × 15-inch jellyroll pan with foil. Grease and lightly flour foil; set aside.

To make soufflé, separate eggs, placing yolks and whites in separate large bowls. Whisk yolks together to blend. Beat whites with cream of tartar until stiff peaks form; set aside.

Place flour, salt, and cayenne on a sheet of waxed paper. Have milk and grated cheese close by. Melt butter in a wide frying pan. Stir in flour, salt, and cayenne and cook for 1 to 2 minutes. Gradually add milk and continue cooking, stirring often, until mixture comes to a boil. Remove from heat and add cheeses, stirring until melted.

Pour cheese mixture into egg yolks and whisk quickly to blend. Fold in ⅓ of the egg whites until combined; then fold in remaining egg whites until blended. Pour into prepared pan, spreading evenly all the way to pan's edge. Bake for 12 to 15 minutes or until surface is puffy and slightly firm.

Have ready a large sheet of foil. When soufflé is done, remove from oven and invert onto foil sheet; carefully peel off greased foil (don't be alarmed if soufflé appears to fall). Set aside to cool slightly.

Spread filling evenly over soufflé and roll up lengthwise, using the foil to help you roll. (You'll notice the edges overlap just slightly.) Place soufflé, seam side down, on a cookie sheet and cover loosely with foil. (Or, wrap in foil and refrigerate overnight; or freeze up to 1 week. When ready to serve, bring to room temperature.)

Preheat oven to 375°. Warm soufflé roll for 15 to 20 minutes while preparing sauce.

To make sauce, melt butter in a wide frying pan. Sauté mushrooms and shallots for 3 to 4 minutes over medium heat, taking care not to let them brown. Stir in flour and cook for 1 to 2 minutes longer. Gradually pour in cream and continue cooking, stirring often, for 3 to 4 minutes or until sauce boils and thickens. Remove from heat and whisk in lemon juice. Season to taste with salt and pepper.

Slice soufflé roll with a long serrated knife and spoon some sauce over each serving. Offer remaining sauce separately.

Makes 10 to 12 servings

At last—a make-ahead dish for a crowd that is also festive enough for the most important entertaining occasions. First you bake a thin, cheese-flavored soufflé in a jellyroll pan. A filling of chicken, spinach, and mushrooms with a hint of Dijon mustard and nutmeg is spread over the soufflé, then it is rolled up and served with a simple sauce combining mushrooms and minced shallots. Both the soufflé and filling may be made in advance and frozen up to 1 week.

Soufflé

7	eggs, room temperature
¼	teaspoon cream of tartar
⅓	cup all-purpose flour
¾	teaspoon salt
⅛	teaspoon cayenne pepper
1¼	cups milk
½	cup grated sharp Cheddar cheese
⅓	cup butter

Sauce

¼	cup butter
2	cups thinly sliced mushrooms
2	tablespoons finely minced shallots
3	tablespoons all-purpose flour
1	cup heavy cream
3	tablespoons lemon juice
	Salt and pepper to taste

Apricot-Mustard Chicken Thighs

½ cup slivered almonds

24 to 30 dried apricots, chopped

12 chicken thighs, boned with skin attached

1 teaspoon salt

1 small onion, finely chopped

¼ cup minced parsley

1¼ cups crème fraîche (page 14) or sour cream

¾ cup apricot preserves

2 tablespoons Dijon mustard

Spread almonds in a shallow baking pan and toast in 350° oven, stirring occasionally, for 3 to 4 minutes until lightly browned. Cool and then finely chop; combine with apricot pieces in a small bowl.

Lay chicken pieces, skin side down, and sprinkle each with salt. Sprinkle a little onion and parsley over each; then spoon a small amount of apricot mixture down the center. Fold chicken skin up and over the filling and fasten edges with toothpicks. (Or, tie each bundle with string.)

Arrange chicken, seam side down, in a shallow baking pan. Increase oven to 400° and bake for 30 to 35 minutes. Remove toothpicks (or string) and arrange on a warm serving platter.

Whisk crème fraîche, apricot preserves, and mustard together in a frying pan over low heat. (Avoid letting sauce come to a boil as it could curdle.) Spoon some hot sauce over chicken bundles to serve. Offer remaining sauce separately.

Makes 6 servings

Boning chicken thighs can be simplified with the aid of a long sharp knife. Since the boned thighs are stuffed and then covered with sauce, the appearance of the chicken isn't very important as long as the skin is left intact. These flavorful bundles of chicken are perfect for a summer buffet along with Jellied Gazpacho (page 44) and Marinated Red Snapper (page 56).

Veal Noisettes in Basil Cream

Melt butter in a wide frying pan over medium heat. Add shallots, basil, mushrooms, and tomatoes. Cook, stirring occasionally, for 3 to 4 minutes. Stir in wine, increase heat, and gently boil until reduced by half. Then whisk in cream and gently boil, stirring occasionally, until reduced by half.

Set mixture aside to cool slightly, then process in a blender or food processor until puréed. Return to pan and whisk in chicken stock. (For a thicker sauce, use less than ½ cup stock.) Cover and refrigerate sauce, if made ahead. Bring to room temperature before using.

Preheat oven to 400°. Trim off any excess fat from veal. Lightly coat sides of meat with softened butter. Place on rack in roasting pan. Cook for 30 to 35 minutes or until meat thermometer registers 160° and meat is browned on outside but still pink inside.

Meanwhile, whisk sauce to blend and reheat just until warm. (Take care not to let sauce come to a full boil.) Spoon a little sauce on each warm dinner plate. Cut veal ¼-inch-thick and arrange overlapping slices of meat on sauce; sprinkle with chives. Offer remaining sauce separately.

Makes 4 servings

3	tablespoons butter
3	large shallots, minced
6	to 8 large basil leaves, chopped
¼	pound mushrooms, sliced
4	to 6 sun-dried tomatoes (page 64, or purchased), cut in thin strips
⅔	cup dry white wine
¾	cup heavy cream
¼	to ½ cup chicken stock
2	veal tenderloins (each about 12 oz.)
	Softened butter
	Chopped chives

Last-minute preparation, especially when it's a reduction sauce, can frazzle even the best cooks. So we've included a delicious party entrée whose full-flavored sauce may be made in advance. We suggest fresh baby carrots (page 29) and rice as accompaniments served with Pinot Noir or Zinfandel.

Herb-stuffed Leg of Lamb

Stuffing

½   cup butter, softened

¼   teaspoon each *dried oregano, sage, mint, rosemary, marjoram, and ground pepper*

1   small bay leaf, crumbled

1   teaspoon salt

1   tablespoon lemon juice

1½   cups soft white bread crumbs

1   leg of lamb (7 lbs.), boned and rolled

     Salt and pepper

2   tablespoons olive oil

Vegetables

1   green pepper, minced

½   cup each *minced carrot, minced onion, and minced celery*

2   cloves garlic, minced

2½   cups beef stock

¼   cup flour mixed with ½ cup water

Combine softened butter, oregano, sage, rosemary, marjoram, mint, pepper, bay leaf, salt, lemon juice and bread crumbs in a bowl; set aside.

Remove string (or casing) from lamb and carefully unroll. Spoon herb stuffing evenly over entire surface. Have kitchen string readily at hand.

Wrapping somewhat tightly, re-roll lamb roast just the way it was. Secure with string in 6 to 8 places. Sprinkle with salt and pepper.

Heat oil in a heavy frying pan and brown roast on all sides, turning often. Transfer to a roasting pan and place in 350° oven for 30 to 35 minutes. Remove from oven and stir pepper, carrots, onion, celery, and garlic into pan juices. Return to oven and cook for 25 to 30 minutes longer or until meat thermometer registers 140° for rare. Lift meat out and set aside; keep warm.

Place roasting pan with pan juices over medium heat; add stock and simmer for 5 minutes. Strain sauce into a medium saucepan, discarding vegetables and skimming off fat. Bring sauce to a boil while whisking in flour paste. Cook until thickened.

Remove strings from meat and thinly slice; arrange on serving platter. Spoon some sauce over top and offer remaining sauce separately.

Makes 8 servings

Serve with Scallop Mousseline with Lemon-Dill Sauce (page 109), glazed carrots (right), and a bottle of Cabernet.

Baby Carrots—Two Methods

Preparation for both recipes begins the same, but then you have a choice between an herb garnish topping or a cognac-flavored glaze.

Cut green tops off carrots, leaving about 1 inch. Peel carrots carefully. Then, using a pair of scissors, trim green stems of each carrot into different lengths until each has a feathery look.

For herb carrots, melt butter in a wide frying pan over medium heat. Add carrots and sauté, stirring occasionally, for 10 to 12 minutes until tender crisp. Season to taste with salt and pepper. Sprinkle with sugar and marjoram and cook for 1 minute. Garnish with minced parsley to serve.

For glazed carrots, melt butter in a wide frying pan over medium heat. Add carrots, salt and pepper to taste, and sugar. Cover and braise, stirring occasionally, for 8 to 10 minutes until tender crisp. Add cognac, shaking pan to coat all sides, and cook for 1 to 2 minutes longer until liquid is absorbed. Serve immediately.

Makes 6 servings

2   bunches (about ¾ lb.) miniature carrots, including green tops

4   tablespoons butter

Salt and freshly ground pepper

1   teaspoon sugar

Pinch dried marjoram

1   tablespoon minced parsley

1   ounce cognac

Miniature vegetables, no matter how simply prepared, add a touch of sophistication to almost any meal. But if baby carrots are hard to find, substitute regular carrots—either diagonally sliced or cut in julienne strips. In both cases, the cooking time would be reduced to 6 to 8 minutes. Glazed carrots can be seen on page 30.

All-white theme for elegant dinner features Scallops in Red Pepper Purée (page 13); light fare features Grilled Halibut with Cucumbers (page 20), Savory Tomato Rice with Pine Nuts (page 32), and Baby Carrots (page 29); early morning basket of fruit and Morning Glory Muffins (page 34).

Savory Tomato Rice with Pine Nuts

2¾ cups chicken stock

1½ cups long-grain white rice (or half brown rice)

3 tablespoons butter

¼ teaspoon salt

Pinch white pepper

¼ cup pine nuts

1 large tomato (seeded and squeezed of excess moisture), finely chopped

3 tablespoons finely minced parsley

1 tablespoon olive oil

2 stalks celery, finely diced

4 green onions (including some tops), thinly sliced

Bring chicken stock to a boil in a medium pan. Stir in rice, 1 tablespoon butter, salt, and white pepper. Cover, reduce heat, and simmer for 20 to 25 minutes or until fluffy.

Meanwhile, spread pine nuts in a wide dry frying pan and place over medium heat, shaking pan often, for 3 to 4 minutes or until golden. Set aside in a small bowl containing tomato and parsley.

Melt remaining 2 tablespoons butter with oil in a frying pan over medium heat. Add celery and cook, stirring occasionally, for 4 to 5 minutes until soft. Add green onions and continue cooking for 1 to 2 minutes longer. Stir in hot cooked rice and the tomato-nut mixture, tossing with a fork to combine. Reheat just to serving temperature as needed.

Makes 6 servings

Pictured on page 30 accompanying Grilled Halibut with Cucumbers (page 20), this flavorful rice compliments any simply-prepared fish or poultry entrée. Try substituting strips of oven-dried tomatoes (page 64) for fresh ones; or use toasted almonds, slivered or whole, in place of the pine nuts. If making rice in advance, cook ingredients and store separately; then stir together and reheat to serve.

Sliced Potatoes & Cheese

Preheat oven to 425°. Lightly butter inside of a shallow, 2-quart baking dish or au gratin pan.

Peel each potato and cut into ¼-inch-thick slices; drop into a bowl of cold water. Let potatoes stand in water until all are prepared. (You should have about 7 cups.) Drain well, blotting excess moisture with paper towels.

Layer ⅓ of the potato slices in prepared pan. Sprinkle with ¼ teaspoon salt, some freshly ground pepper, ⅓ of the onion, and ⅓ of the cheese. Dot with 1 tablespoon butter. Repeat layering 2 more times.

Combine stock and wine; pour into pan down the sides, but not directly over the potatoes. Cover and bake for 15 minutes. Remove cover and return to oven for 45 to 50 minutes longer or until top is golden brown and bubbly. Remove from oven and allow to set for 5 minutes. Sprinkle with parsley to serve.

Makes 4 to 6 servings

2½	pounds white potatoes
¾	teaspoon salt
	Freshly ground pepper
½	cup thinly sliced green onion (including some tops)
2	cups (8 oz.) shredded Gruyère or Swiss cheese
3	tablespoons butter
½	cup chicken stock
⅓	cup dry white wine
	Minced parsley

Morning Glory Muffins

2	cups all-purpose flour
2	teaspoons ground cinnamon
2	teaspoons baking soda
½	teaspoon salt
1¼	cups sugar
1½	cups finely shredded carrots
2	large tart apples, peeled and shredded
½	cup raisins
¾	cup shredded coconut
½	cup chopped pecans
3	lightly beaten eggs
1	cup vegetable oil
½	teaspoon vanilla

Preheat oven to 375°. Grease muffin tins with shortening; set aside.

Sift flour with cinnamon, baking soda, and salt into a large bowl. Stir in sugar until blended. Then add carrots, apples, raisins, coconut, and pecans until blended. Make a well in center of mixture and pour in eggs, oil, and vanilla all at once. Stir just until mixture is evenly moist.

Spoon batter into muffin tins, filling at least ¾ full (almost to the top). Bake for 18 to 20 minutes or until golden. Serve warm.

Makes 20 to 24 muffins

These moist, hearty muffins are perfect for a late morning breakfast accompanied by wedges of ripe melon and the season's first strawberries as pictured in an outdoor setting on page 30.

Layered Lemon Pie

Combine flour, sugar, and salt in a food processor. Add butter, lard, and shortening and whirl for 8 to 10 seconds until mixture has the consistency of cornmeal. With motor running, add the ice water, a tablespoon at a time, until a ball is formed. Turn out onto a sheet of waxed paper and flatten into a smooth disc. Roll out on a floured board to a thickness of ⅛-inch. Fit into a 9-inch pie pan and refrigerate for 30 minutes.

Preheat oven to 425°. Prick bottom and sides of pastry shell with a fork. Lay a sheet of foil loosely inside and fill with pie weights (or beans). Bake for 8 to 10 minutes. Remove foil and weights, reduce oven to 375°, and return for 5 to 8 minutes longer or until golden.

Meanwhile, melt butter in top of a double boiler positioned over simmering water. Add lemon zest, lemon juice, sugar, eggs, and egg yolks, whisking to combine. Cook, stirring often, for 10 to 15 minutes until thickened. Set aside to cool completely.

Spread half the ice cream into pie shell. Cover with half the filling; repeat layering again. Cover loosely with plastic wrap and freeze for several hours until firm. (Or wrap frozen pie in foil and store in freezer for 2 weeks.)

Preheat oven to 475°. Whip egg whites until soft peaks form. Slowly add sugar and whip until stiff peaks form. Spread meringue over top of frozen pie, taking care to cover entire surface and seal the edges. Bake for 3 to 5 minutes, checking every 30 seconds for browning, until meringue is lightly browned. Refrigerate up to 15 minutes before serving. (Or, return to freezer for up to 8 hours.)

Makes about 8 servings

Dough

1⅓	cups all-purpose flour
1	teaspoon sugar
¼	teaspoon salt
¼	cup cold unsalted butter
2	tablespoons lard (or solid shortening)
2	tablespoons shortening
2	to 3 tablespoons ice water

Filling

6	tablespoons butter
1½	tablespoons grated lemon zest
⅓	cup fresh lemon juice
1	cup sugar
2	lightly beaten eggs
2	egg yolks
1	quart vanilla ice cream, softened
6	egg whites, room temperature
½	cup sugar

Lemon Macaroon Torte

Meringue Paste

1   can (8 oz.) almond paste

1   cup sugar

2   egg whites (¼ cup)

Pastry Cream

3   egg yolks

½   cup sugar

⅓   cup all-purpose flour

1   cup hot milk

2   teaspoons butter

1   teaspoon vanilla

Preheat oven to 325°. Trace two 8-inch circles on two sheets of parchment paper and place on separate cookie sheets; set aside.

Using an electric mixer, beat almond paste, sugar, and egg whites on medium speed for 3 to 5 minutes until smooth. (Or whirl in food processor for 1 minute.) Scoop mixture into a large pastry bag fitted with a large star tip (No. 7 or larger). Pipe a continuous single ring of paste mixture around the inside circumference of one of the parchment circles. (You should use about ¾ of the dough for this ring.)

Pipe remaining dough on other parchment circle. Using a spatula or wide knife, spread dough evenly to a thickness of about ¼-inch, covering the circle completely.

Place both baking sheets in the preheated oven and bake, removing solid bottom layer after 18 to 20 minutes and ring-shaped top layer after 20 to 25 minutes. Cool on racks for about 30 minutes; then invert and carefully pull off parchment paper. Allow shells to rest upside down (sticky-side-up) until ready to use.

To make pastry cream, whisk egg yolks and sugar together for about 5 minutes or until mixture turns light in color and reaches the ribbon stage when tested. (Mixture should form a trail or ribbon across the surface when the whisk is lifted.) Stir in flour until incorporated. Then add hot milk slowly, whisking all the time until combined.

Transfer mixture to a heavy saucepan and cook over medium heat, whisking constantly, until sauce comes to a boil and thickens. Reduce heat and let cream continue to bubble, stirring occasionally, for 2 to 3 minutes longer. Remove from heat and stir in butter and vanilla; set aside to cool while preparing filling.

To make filling, combine sugar, cornstarch, and water in a heavy, medium-size saucepan over medium heat. Bring to a boil, whisking continuously to prevent lumps. Remove from heat. Whisk egg yolks together in a small bowl; add a little of the hot sugar mixture, stirring to combine. Return egg-sugar mixture to saucepan and cook, stirring constantly, for about 1 minute or until it comes to a full boil. Remove from heat. Add butter, lemon juice, and zest, and stir. Set aside to cool.

To assemble, place bottom shell, sticky-side-up, on a serving platter. Spread about 1 cup pastry cream evenly over the top, coming all the way to the edges. Position top shell over the cream and align edges. Fill center area with ⅔ of the lemon filling. Sprinkle some almonds decoratively over the top and dust only the edges of the shell with powdered sugar. Refrigerate at least 1 hour before serving.

Makes 8 servings

Filling

1	*cup sugar*
¼	*cup cornstarch*
1	*cup water*
3	*egg yolks*
2	*tablespoons butter*
⅓	*cup lemon juice*
2	*to 3 tablespoons grated lemon zest*
⅓	*cup sliced almonds*
	Sifted powdered sugar

Bake the meringue shell and store at room temperature if made ahead. The pastry cream and the filling can be made a day in advance too and refrigerated until you're ready to assemble the dessert. Excess pastry cream may be frozen up to 2 weeks. For our dessert sampling, pictured on pages 10 and 11, we shaped Lemon Macaroon Torte into a rectangle measuring 6 by 14 inches and used the entire recipe of lemon filling.

Strawberry Cream Cake

Cake

⅓   cup sugar

3   eggs, room temperature

½   cup all-purpose flour

½   teaspoon vanilla

1½   tablespoons melted sweet butter

Syrup

⅓   cup sugar

⅓   cup water

1½   tablespoons kirsch

⅔   cup raspberry jam

Preheat oven to 350°. Generously grease a 9-inch round cake pan with butter. Dust with flour, shaking out excess.

Place sugar and eggs in a medium-size bowl positioned over a large bowl of hot water. Whisk continuously for 1 minute. Remove and then beat on high speed with electric mixer for 2 to 3 minutes. Decrease speed to low and continue beating for 5 minutes or until mixture is pale in color and falls from beater in a steady ribbon.

Fold in flour until combined. Mix vanilla with warm butter and stir into batter just until incorporated. Pour into prepared pan and bake for 25 to 30 minutes or until cake is golden brown and pulls away from the sides of pan. Cool for 10 minutes before turning out onto a rack to cool completely. Don't worry if cake appears no more than an inch high; it is supposed to be thin. (At this point, cake may be wrapped and stored in refrigerator for 3 days, or frozen up to 1 month.)

To make syrup, combine sugar and water in a heavy saucepan over medium heat. Bring to a boil, stirring to dissolve sugar. Remove from heat, cool, and stir in kirsch.

Slice cake horizontally into 2 equal layers using a long serrated knife. (Don't be too concerned if layers aren't exactly even—it won't show.) Place one layer, cut side up, on serving platter. Brush cut surface with all the syrup; then spread evenly with jam. Set aside to prepare filling.

Whip cream in a medium-size bowl on high speed until stiff peaks form; set aside.

In a small bowl, sprinkle gelatin over cold water. Position bowl over a larger bowl filled with boiling water and swirl gelatin until dissolved.

To make filling, in a large bowl, beat cream cheese and sugar together until fluffy. Stir in gelatin; fold in whipped cream just until blended. Spread an even layer of filling, ½ to 1-inch thick, over raspberry jam. Position top layer of cake, cut side down, over filling and press down slightly.

Using a flexible metal spatula, spread a very thin layer of filling around sides and top of cake. Then frost entire cake with a second, slightly thicker layer while rotating the cake and smoothing the sides evenly as you go.

Scoop remaining cream into a pastry bag fitted with a ½-inch tip. Pipe a decorative border along top edge of cake (see photograph on page 11). Refrigerate for 3 hours (or as long as overnight).

To make glaze, warm currant jelly in a small saucepan until liquefied; cool slightly. Stir in kirsch. Place 12 to 15 of the choicest strawberries in a bowl. Pour over currant glaze, swirling bowl to coat berries completely. Remove and drain, hull-sides-down, on a plate for 1 minute. (This prevents dripping or the possibility of staining the cream with excess glaze.)

Arrange berries, close together and with hull-sides-down, inside the cream border on top of cake. Chill for 1 hour.

Slice remaining berries into a serving bowl and offer with slices of cake.

Makes 8 servings

Filling

3	cups heavy cream, well chilled
1	tablespoon unflavored gelatin
2	tablespoons cold water
8	ounces cream cheese, softened
⅓	cup sugar

Glaze

¼	cup red currant jelly
1	tablespoon kirsch
3	baskets (12 oz.) strawberries, hulled

When the season's first strawberries appear, we think you'll be eager to try this wonderful dessert as a finale to a special meal.

Chocolate Mousse Torte

Softened butter

Crust

3   *cups (13 oz.) crushed chocolate wafers*

½   *cup melted sweet butter*

Filling

1   *pound semi-sweet chocolate*

2   *whole eggs*

4   *eggs, separated*

2   *cups heavy cream*

6   *tablespoons powdered sugar*

Chocolate Leaves

6   *ounces semi-sweet chocolate*

1   *tablespoon shortening*

8   *to 10 camellia leaves*

1   *cup heavy cream*

    Sugar

Heavily grease bottom and sides of a 10-inch springform pan with softened butter.

Combine cookie crumbs with melted butter in a small bowl. Lightly press into bottom and completely up the sides of prepared pan. Refrigerate for 30 minutes.

Meanwhile, break chocolate into pieces and melt in top of double boiler over simmering water. Remove and set aside to cool slightly; then pour into a large bowl and stir in whole eggs. Add egg yolks, whisking until blended.

Whip cream with powdered sugar until soft peaks form. Beat egg whites until stiff (but not dry) peaks form. Fold a little whipped cream and some egg whites into chocolate mixture to lighten. Fold in remaining cream and whites just until blended.

Pour into crust-lined pan, cover, and refrigerate for at least 6 hours or overnight.

To make chocolate leaves, break chocolate into pieces and melt with shortening in top of double boiler over simmering water. Wash and thoroughly dry camellia leaves. Using a spoon, coat the underside of each leaf with chocolate. Make sure the chocolate is thick enough or it will break when separated from the camellia leaf. Place leaves on a sheet of waxed paper and chill (or freeze) until set.

Whip remaining 1 cup cream with sugar to taste until stiff peaks form. Loosen crust from pan on all sides with a knife; release spring and remove rim. Spread half the cream over top of cake and pipe remaining cream into rosettes with a pastry bag. Carefully separate chocolate and camellia leaves. Arrange chocolate ones around rosettes.

Cut in wedges to serve.

Makes 10 servings

Thoughts for Entertaining

Springtime brings a fresh promise of sunshine and flowers . . .

What better reason to have a party than to share the beauty of your garden.

Pretty goblets holding a single spectacular rose or camellia add beauty to any table. If set at each place, use a bright ribbon to attach a placecard around the stem of each glass.

To extend a centerpiece, use trailing ribbons, ivy, clematis, jasmine, or violets; or scatter flower petals or crystal beads down the center of the table.

To highlight colorful Easter eggs and candies, try growing "grass" in a shallow container (see directions at right).

Construct a parsley hedge and cut vegetable flowers for an hors d'oeuvres table centerpiece. Wedge tall sprigs of parsley into a long, narrow container. Use canapé cutters to cut varying sizes of flowers from thin slices of carrot, beet, jícama, turnip, and English cucumber. Layer together, place on bamboo skewers, and arrange in the hedge.

When giving a shower, paint plastic watering cans, fill them with flowers, and hang them on your door. Decorate the table with colorfully wrapped boxes.

To lengthen the life of your flower arrangement, select your flowers 24 hours in advance. Condition them by snipping the stems and placing in deep water.

Sow your own Easter "grass" using vermiculite and wheat seed in proportions of three-to-one. Spread vermiculite in a shallow container. Sprinkle seed over, either covering surface completely or in a pattern. Water well—almost to running over. Cover with plastic wrap for 2 days or until seeds germinate. Remove plastic and seeds will grow about 3 inches in 7 days. The more you cut it, the thicker it will become.

SUMMER

Taste the Seasons

Clockwise from top: feline resident at Guild; delphiniums and wax flowers arranged in antique French tole coffee urn; Cold Curry Soup (page 45) served in Court of Abundance; terra cotta roof tiles of original building; blue wrought iron furniture, a trademark at Allied Arts.

Jellied Gazpacho

Mayonnaise

2   egg yolks

1   teaspoon each *dry mustard and salt*

Worcestershire

Paprika

1   tablespoon boiling water

1   cup cold salad oil

1   tablespoon each lemon juice and vinegar

Gelatin

1   large can (20 oz.) tomato-vegetable juice

2   envelopes unflavored gelatin

4   medium tomatoes, seeded and chopped

1   small onion, chopped

½   green pepper, diced

1   stalk celery, diced

1   cucumber, peeled, seeded, and diced

1   clove garlic, minced

¼   cup red wine vinegar

3   dashes Tabasco

¼   cup olive oil

To make mayonnaise, whirl egg yolks, mustard, salt, a few drops of Worcestershire, and paprika in a blender or food processor. With motor running, add the 1 tablespoon boiling water. Then, begin to add the cold salad oil, a few drops in the beginning. As mayonnaise begins to thicken (after adding half the oil), pour in the lemon juice and vinegar. (This thins the mayonnaise somewhat.) Slowly add remaining ½ cup oil until incorporated. Cover and refrigerate until serving time.

Heat vegetable juice in a small saucepan until warm. Transfer to a bowl, sprinkle gelatin on top, and set aside to dissolve.

Stir in tomatoes, onion, green pepper, celery, cucumber, garlic, vinegar, Tabasco, and oil until blended well.

Pour into a 9 × 13-inch glass or ceramic baking dish. Chill for at least 4 hours or overnight.

To serve, cut gazpacho into squares or rectangles, as desired. Arrange a few butter lettuce leaves on each chilled salad plate. Center a portion of gazpacho on lettuce and garnish with a dollop of fresh mayonnaise.

Makes 6 to 8 servings

For a more festive presentation, spoon about ¾ cup of the gazpacho mixture into 1-cup custard cups or decorative molds that have been sprayed with vegetable spray and chill as directed. Serve with thin slices of avocado.

Cold Curry Soup with Apricot Cream

Melt butter in a wide frying pan over medium heat. Add onions and celery and cook, stirring occasionally, for 6 to 8 minutes until vegetables are soft. Reduce heat to low, stir in flour and the 1 tablespoon curry powder. Cook, stirring often, for 3 to 4 minutes more.

Transfer vegetable mixture to blender or food processor. Add apples and 1 cup stock. Whirl until smooth; then return mixture to a large pot. Add remaining chicken stock and bay leaf. Bring to a gentle boil and then reduce heat and simmer, uncovered, for 5 minutes. Remove bay leaf and season to taste with salt and pepper. Set aside to cool; then cover and chill for 4 to 6 hours to blend flavors.

Meanwhile, combine apricots and water in a small saucepan. Bring to a boil over moderate heat and cook for 10 minutes. Transfer to a blender or food processor and whirl until smooth. Add sugar and lemon juice and whirl to combine. Set aside to cool. Simmer Port in a small saucepan over medium heat until reduced by half. Stir in apricot purée and remaining 2 teaspoons curry powder. Simmer, uncovered, for 5 minutes; remove from heat and set aside to cool.

Whip cream in a small bowl until stiff peaks form. Fold in cooled apricot purée and transfer to a small bowl. Ladle soup into wide bowls and top each with a dollop of apricot cream. Offer remaining cream separately.

Makes 6 servings

½	cup butter
2	onions, coarsely chopped
3	stalks celery, strings removed and sliced
2	tablespoons all-purpose flour
1	tablespoon curry powder
2	tart apples, peeled, cored and chopped
8	cups chicken stock
1	bay leaf
	Salt and white pepper

Topping

½	cup dried apricots
½	cup water
¼	cup superfine sugar
½	teaspoon lemon juice
1	cup Port
2	teaspoons curry powder
½	cup heavy cream

This refreshing curry-flavored soup is the perfect choice for mid-summer entertaining as pictured on pages 42 and 43.

Chilled Cucumber & Yogurt Soup

1	medium English cucumber
1	avocado (such as Haas or Fuerte)
4	green onions (including some tops), chopped
1⅓	cups chicken stock
½	cup sour cream
½	cup yogurt
2	teaspoons minced fresh dill (or ½ teaspoon dried dillweed)
¼	teaspoon garlic powder
	Salt and freshly ground pepper
	Sprigs of dill

Cut unpeeled cucumber in half lengthwise and scoop out the seeds. Cut 12 paper thin slices of cucumber and reserve for garnish. Coarsely chop remaining cucumber and set aside.

Peel avocado and cut into chunks, dropping pieces into a blender or food processor. Whirl until puréed. Add cucumbers, onion, chicken stock, sour cream, yogurt, dill, and garlic powder (in batches, if necessary) and whirl until smooth. Season to taste with salt and pepper. Cover and refrigerate until well chilled.

Ladle soup into shallow rimmed soup bowls and garnish each serving with sprigs of fresh dill and 3 half slices of cucumber.

Makes 4 servings

"Cool and refreshing" best describes this make-ahead soup that combines the mild flavors of cucumber, avocado, and fresh dill. Serve well chilled as a first course, followed by Seafood Pasta Salad (page 54) for a light meal on a warm summer evening. Your favorite fruit ice or our strawberry-flavored sorbet (page 69) complete the menu.

Minted Pea Soup

Melt butter in a large, heavy saucepan over medium heat. Add onion and sauté for 2 to 3 minutes or until soft. Stir in peas, chicken stock, and salt. Measure savory into the palm of your hand. Crumble between your thumb and forefinger and drop into soup.

Bring soup to a boil, cover, reduce heat, and simmer for 30 minutes. Cool slightly, then place in a blender or food processor, in batches if necessary, and whirl until smooth.

Pour soup through a strainer to make extra smooth and creamy. Stir mint into the soup.

Cover and refrigerate for at least 4 hours or until well chilled. Stir in half-and-half just before serving and garnish each serving with tiny mint leaves.

Makes about 8 servings

2	tablespoons butter
1	large onion, thinly sliced
2	packages (16 oz. each) tiny frozen peas
5	cups chicken stock
2	teaspoons salt
2½	teaspoons summer savory
2	tablespoons finely chopped fresh mint leaves
1	cup half-and-half
	Sprigs of mint

For a special presentation, serve Minted Pea Soup in glass bowls with ice liners to keep it really cold. It's a wonderful first course with a Sauvignon Blanc, followed by Grilled Tuna with Lemon-Tarragon Sauce (page 57) and Fruit with Ice Cream & Crème Anglaise (page 70). Fresh mint is essential in this recipe—if it's not available, we suggest waiting for a more seasonal time. We recommend not freezing this soup.

Savory Summer Salad

Vinaigrette

2   tablespoons Dijon
    mustard

¼   cup red wine vinegar

⅓   cup olive oil

1   tablespoon minced
    shallots

1   tablespoon capers,
    drained

½   cup chopped fresh
    basil

    Salt and freshly
    ground pepper

3   large tomatoes, peeled
    and seeded

3   avocados

    Butter lettuce

Combine mustard, vinegar, oil, shallots, capers, and basil in a small saucepan. Place over low heat until just simmering. Season to taste with salt and pepper.

Cut tomatoes into thick slices, then cut slices in half. Peel, pit, and slice avocados. Arrange both attractively on individual glass salad plates that have been lined with a few butter lettuce leaves.

Spoon warm dressing over each serving.

Makes 6 servings

The nice thing about this salad is that it goes with almost everything—grilled fish or chicken, barbecued beef such as flank steak or chateaubriand, even pasta or meatless entrées. Vine-ripe tomatoes and full-flavored avocados, such as Hass or Fuerte, are essential ingredients for Savory Summer Salad.

Beets & Feta Cheese with Endive

Cut off tops of the beets (reserve for other uses, see below). Wrap beets in foil and bake in a 350° oven for 50 to 60 minutes or until just tender.

Meanwhile, place walnuts in a wide dry frying pan and toast over medium heat, shaking pan constantly, for 1 to 2 minutes. Set aside.

Remove beets from oven and when cool enough to handle, peel and dice into ½-inch cubes. Place in a small bowl.

Whisk together vinegar and mustard; slowly add oil, a little at a time, until well blended. Season to taste with salt and pepper.

Pour half of the dressing over the beets, tossing to combine.

To serve, arrange endive leaves on a serving platter in a spoke-like fashion. Mound beets in the center and drizzle remaining dressing over the top. Sprinkle with crumbled cheese and walnuts; serve immediately.

Makes 8 servings

2	bunches beets (about 3½ lbs.)
½	cup (2 oz.) walnuts, coarsely chopped
¼	cup red wine vinegar
1	teaspoon Dijon mustard
¾	cup walnut oil (or fruity olive oil)
	Salt and freshly ground pepper
3	bunches, Belgian endive, washed
4	ounces feta cheese, crumbled

Beet tops may be steamed over boiling water for a few minutes until tender in a similar way to preparing fresh spinach. Toss with a little tarragon vinegar and butter to serve. We think our beet and feta cheese salad goes particularly well with any simply grilled meat or as a colorful addition to a summer buffet table.

Cobb Salad

Dressing

1⅓   cups salad oil

⅔   cup white vinegar

1   clove garlic, minced

1   teaspoon each *salt, sugar, paprika, dry mustard, and Worcestershire*

½   teaspoon pepper

½   head iceberg lettuce, finely chopped

½   bunch watercress, finely chopped

1   small bunch chicory, finely chopped

2   to 3 tablespoons snipped chives

3   small tomatoes, finely chopped

2   to 3 cups cooked chicken, diced

8   slices bacon, crisply cooked and crumbled

2   hard-cooked eggs, chopped

3   ounces blue cheese, crumbled

1   avocado

Combine oil, vinegar, garlic, salt, sugar, paprika, mustard, Worcestershire, and pepper in a jar. Cover and refrigerate. (It will keep for several days.)

Place lettuce, watercress, chicory, chives, tomatoes, chicken, bacon, eggs, and blue cheese in a salad bowl. (At this point, you may refrigerate for up to 6 hours.)

To serve, peel, pit, and dice avocado and add to the salad. Pour over some of the dressing and toss to combine. Serve immediately and offer remaining dressing separately.

Makes 6 to 8 servings

Everyone enjoys a good Cobb salad. It's attractive and delicious tasting plus it can be prepared hours in advance—perfect for entertaining large groups, too. Warm French rolls or sourdough bread and Chenin Blanc complete the menu.

Pasta Salad Niçoise

Whisk together oil and vinegar in a small bowl; add capers, basil, marjoram, oregano, thyme, garlic, salt, and pepper.

Cook pasta in boiling salted water until *al dente* (still slightly firm to the bite). Rinse, drain well, and place in a large bowl. Blanch green beans in boiling water for 3 to 5 minutes; plunge into cold water to stop the cooking process and drain.

To assemble, toss pasta with half the dressing. Place a small mound attractively on each serving plate. Arrange some tuna, a few beans, pepper strips, onion slices, tomatoes, and olives on each plate. Sprinkle with parsley and garnish each with a sprig of herb. Offer remaining dressing separately at the table.

Makes 6 to 8 servings

Pictured on page 62. Arrange ingredients on glass plates for an attractive presentation. You may refrigerate up to 4 hours; allow salad to come to room temperature to serve. Remember, Greek olives—available at delicatessens and in gourmet sections of most markets—rarely come pitted! You may want to substitute pitted ripe olives. For more flavor, marinate them first in a rich vinaigrette with lots of garlic. You can substitute ¾ teaspoon dried herbs for each of the fresh ones.

Dressing

¾	*cup olive oil*
⅓	*cup white wine vinegar*
1½	*tablespoons capers*
1½	*tablespoons each chopped fresh basil, marjoram, oregano, and thyme*
2	*cloves garlic, minced*
¼	*teaspoon salt*
	Ground pepper
7	*ounces spinach pasta*
½	*pound green beans*
1	*small red pepper, seeded and cut in strips*
1	*small red onion, sliced paper thin*
18	*to 24 Greek olives*
1	*can tuna, drained*
3	*tomatoes, cut in wedges*
2	*tablespoons minced parsley*
	Sprigs of fresh herbs

Marinated Beef Salad

Dressing

¼   cup red wine vinegar

1   teaspoon each *lemon juice, dry mustard, and salt*

½   teaspoon each *dried tarragon and Worcestershire*

1   tablespoon soy sauce

½   teaspoon pepper

¾   cup salad oil

½   pound snow peas

1   tablespoon butter

¼   pound mushrooms, sliced

3   large cooked potatoes, peeled and diced

1   red pepper, cut in julienne strips

1   red onion, diced

¾   cup each *chopped dill pickle and diced celery*

2   tablespoons minced parsley

1   pound cooked roast beef, cut in julienne strips

Sprigs of parsley

Whisk together vinegar, lemon juice, mustard, salt, tarragon, Worcestershire, soy, and ground pepper in a small bowl. Slowly whisk in oil. Cover and refrigerate.

Trim and discard strings and tips from snow peas. Steam peas over boiling water for 2 to 3 minutes until tender crisp. Plunge into cold water to stop the cooking process. Drain well and then wrap in plastic and refrigerate to keep crisp.

Melt butter in a small frying pan. Add mushrooms and sauté over medium-high heat for 2 to 3 minutes until golden. Remove with a slotted spoon and place in a bowl along with potatoes, red pepper, onion, dill pickle, celery, and parsley. Pour over half the dressing and toss gently; chill for 30 minutes.

Arrange some pieces of beef and a few snow peas decoratively down one side of each salad plate. Spoon some vegetable mixture into a large mound near the center of the plate and garnish other side with sprigs of parsley. Spoon remaining dressing over the meat and snow peas.

Makes 6 servings

The roast beef—either purchased from a delicatessen or leftover from a recent barbecue—can be thinly sliced rather than cut in julienne strips, if preferred. Roll the slices cornucopia-style and arrange them on one side of the plate.

New Potato Salad with Roquefort

Whisk together vinegar, shallots, mustard, salt, and pepper in a small bowl. Add oil slowly, a few drops at a time and whisk continuously, until smooth. Add parsley and set aside.

Cook potatoes in boiling salted water for 20 minutes or until just tender. While still warm, slice thinly into a bowl. Whisk vinaigrette to combine and then pour half of the dressing over potatoes. Toss gently, taking care not to break too many slices.

Arrange lettuce leaves on a serving platter. Using a fork, arrange overlapping slices of potato in long, even rows, across the bed of lettuce. Arrange watercress between rows of potatoes.

Stir Roquefort, cream, and half the crumbled bacon into remaining vinaigrette. Spoon some over potatoes. Sprinkle remaining bacon and chives over the top. Offer remaining vinaigrette separately.

Makes 6 to 8 servings

We enjoy serving this full-flavored salad warm or at room temperature but preferably not chilled. Its special presentation makes it a winner. For accompaniments, we suggest any simply grilled meat or chicken and steamed seasonal vegetables.

Vinaigrette

3	tablespoons tarragon vinegar
¼	cup finely chopped shallots
1	teaspoon Dijon mustard
¾	teaspoon salt
½	teaspoon freshly ground pepper
½	cup olive oil
2	tablespoons minced parsley
2	pounds small new potatoes
1	small head leafy lettuce, such as butter
¼	to ½ bunch watercress
2	to 4 tablespoons crumbled Roquefort
½	cup heavy cream
10	strips (½ lb.) bacon, crisply cooked and crumbled
2	tablespoons snipped chives

Seafood Pasta Salad

1¼ *pounds medium shrimp, shelled and deveined*

¾ *pound bay scallops*

4 *to 6 small squid, cleaned (optional)*

½ *pound pasta, such as twists or shells*

1 *cup tiny frozen peas, thawed and drained*

1 *medium red pepper, seeded and cut into thin julienne strips*

½ *cup minced red onion*

Dressing

½ *cup pesto (recipe at right, or purchased)*

3 *tablespoons lemon juice*

1 *teaspoon Dijon mustard*

¼ *teaspoon salt*

¼ *teaspoon pepper*

½ *cup olive oil*

1 *cup imported black olives*

Fill a 3-quart pan with water and bring to a boil. Drop in shrimp and scallops and cook for just 1 minute. (Avoid overcooking!) Remove immediately, rinse in cold water to stop the cooking process, and drain.

Cut bodies of squid into ½-inch-thick rings and cut tentacles in half. Drop pieces into boiling water and simmer for 5 minutes. Drain well.

Meanwhile, cook pasta in boiling salted water until *al dente* (still slightly firm to the bite). Drain, rinse in cold water, and drain again. Place in a large bowl along with shrimp, scallops, squid, peas, red pepper, and onion. Toss gently to combine.

Combine ½ cup pesto with lemon juice, mustard, salt, and pepper in a small bowl. Slowly whisk in olive oil until combined. Pour over salad and toss well. Serve on individual salad plates topped with a generous sprinkling of olives.

Makes 6 to 8 servings

Homemade pesto is so simple to make you may never go back to buying it again. Combine 4 cups fresh basil leaves, 5 cloves garlic, 3 tablespoons olive oil, and ¼ cup grated Parmesan cheese in a food processor. Whirl until well chopped but not completely puréed. (You may have to do this in batches.) Store unused portion in a jar. Cover top surface with a thin film of olive oil to prevent discoloration. (Or freeze in an airtight container up to 3 months.)

Taste the Seasons

Pasta with Scallops & Pea Pods

Melt 1 tablespoon butter in a frying pan over medium heat. Add mushrooms and sauté for 3 to 5 minutes until limp; remove and set aside.

Steam pea pods over boiling water for 2 minutes until tender crisp. Plunge into cold water to stop the cooking process. Drain and set aside.

Meanwhile, cook pasta in boiling salted water until *al dente* (still firm to the bite).

Combine scallops, vermouth, wine, water, bay leaf, and thyme in a shallow pan and place over medium heat. When liquid comes to its first boil (about 1½ minutes), remove from heat. Drain scallops and transfer to a warm dish.

Meanwhile, melt remaining 4 tablespoons butter in a wide frying pan. Add garlic, cream, cheese, and salt and pepper to taste, whisking until hot and smooth. Return pea pods, mushrooms, and scallops to sauce and heat through.

Arrange hot pasta on a serving platter and spoon sauce over top. Scatter strips of tomato over and serve immediately. Offer additional grated cheese separately.

Makes 6 servings

It's important to have all the ingredients readily at hand since the dish goes together quickly. Try substituting a vegetable pasta for plain pasta. Many specialty shops and delicatessens offer such varieties as: spinach, red pepper, herb and tomato-flavored ones.

5	*tablespoons butter*
½	*pound mushrooms, thinly sliced*
⅓	*pound Chinese pea pods, trimmed*
1	*pound fettucine or flavored pasta*
1¼	*to 1½ pounds bay scallops*
½	*cup dry vermouth*
½	*cup dry white wine*
⅓	*cup water*
1	*bay leaf*
	Sprig of thyme
3	*cloves garlic, minced*
1	*cup heavy cream*
¾	*cup freshly grated Parmesan cheese*
	Salt and white pepper
	Thin strips of Oven-dried Tomato (page 64)
	Grated Parmesan cheese

Marinated Red Snapper

4 tablespoons clarified butter (see right)

2 pounds red snapper fillets, or other firm-textured fish

Marinade

2 tablespoons cider vinegar

¼ cup orange juice

2 tablespoons orange zest

2 tablespoons minced shallots

2 tablespoons minced green pepper

½ teaspoon salt

¼ teaspoon cayenne pepper

½ cup olive oil

Thin slices of orange

Sprigs of cilantro

To keep butter from burning while sautéing fish, it should be clarified first. Cut butter into pieces and melt in a small saucepan over low heat. When completely melted, turn off heat and set aside to cool as you skim off any foam floating on top.

As butter cools, it separates into a clear liquid on top and a sediment on the bottom. Carefully, pour the transparent liquid into another pan or small dish. This clarified butter is now ready for use. (Figure about 5 tablespoons of butter are needed to produce 4 tablespoons clarified butter.)

Place 4 tablespoons clarified butter in a wide frying pan over medium high heat. Add fish fillets, a few at a time, and sauté, turning once so as to brown both sides, for no more than 1 to 2 minutes per side. (Longer cooking will cause fish to fall apart.)

Carefully, lift out fish, making sure fillets remain whole, and transfer to a large platter or flat baking dish.

Combine vinegar, orange juice, zest, shallots, green pepper, salt, and cayenne. Whisk in oil until blended. Pour over fish; cover and refrigerate for at least 6 hours or overnight, basting occasionally with marinade accumulating in bottom of pan.

To serve, lift fish from marinade and arrange on serving platter. Garnish with slices of orange and sprigs of cilantro.

Makes 6 servings

Grilled Tuna with Lemon-Tarragon Sauce

Whisk together oil, wine, parsley, and tarragon. Wipe each fish fillet with a damp cloth and then coat both sides with some of the baste.

Lightly grease the barbecue grill (or stovetop grill) with oil. Arrange fish on hot grill, positioned 4 to 6 inches above a solid bed of low-glowing coals. Grill, turning once to brown both sides, for 8 to 10 minutes (4 to 5 minutes per side). Fish should appear flaky near the thickest part.

Meanwhile, combine vinegar, shallots, lemon juice, and tarragon in a small pan over medium-high heat. Cook quickly until reduced to about 2 tablespoons. Remove from heat and whisk in 2 or 3 pieces of butter until melted.

Turn temperature to medium-low and return pan to heat. Continue to add butter, a couple of pieces at a time, whisking continuously until all the butter has been incorporated and the sauce has the consistency of light mayonnaise.

Arrange fish on warm dinner plates and spoon some sauce over fillet to serve. Garnish with lemon.

Makes 6 servings

The sauce may be prepared first and kept warm in a wide-mouthed thermos while grilling fish. The smoke from mesquite or other hardwood charcoal can transform any grilled fish into one with distinct flavor. Scatter a handful of pre-soaked (in water) pieces of mesquite over glowing coals and allow them to smolder a bit. Then grill as directed. (Avoid any chemically-treated briquettes.)

Baste

½	cup olive oil
2	tablespoons dry white wine
2	tablespoons minced parsley
¼	teaspoon dried tarragon
6	tuna fillets (each cut 1-inch thick), or other firm-textured fish such as halibut

Sauce

⅓	cup tarragon vinegar
¼	cup minced shallots
2	tablespoons fresh lemon juice
¼	teaspoon dried tarragon
1	cup (½ lb.) butter, room temperature and cut in 16 pieces

Thin slices of lemon

Spinach-stuffed Chicken Breasts

Stuffing

2   tablespoons butter

3   green onions (including some tops), thinly sliced

1   package frozen spinach, thawed and squeezed of excess moisture

1   lightly beaten egg

½   cup ricotta cheese

⅓   cup pesto (page 54)

4   thin slices prosciutto, finely chopped

3   chicken breasts, split and boned

    Melted butter

4   tablespoons grated Parmesan cheese

Lightly butter a shallow baking dish and set aside.

Melt butter in a wide frying pan over medium heat. Add onions and sauté for 2 to 3 minutes until soft. Stir in spinach until combined. Remove from heat and set aside.

Combine egg, ricotta, pesto, and prosciutto in a medium-size bowl. Stir in spinach mixture, tossing to combine.

Place one half chicken breast on a flat work surface. With skin side up, loosen skin from one side of the breast, forming a pocket underneath. Spoon about 3 tablespoons stuffing into the pocket, then tuck skin under breast, forming a neat even bundle. Repeat for remaining breasts.

Dip each bundle into melted butter and carefully roll in grated cheese, taking care not to let stuffing come out. Place in a prepared pan.

Bake in a 350° oven for about 30 minutes or until chicken is golden brown and heated through. Or, serve cold or at room temperature, if desired.

Makes 6 servings

We've pictured Spinach-stuffed Chicken Breasts on page 63 with suggested accompaniments, but we think this versatile recipe goes well with almost anything. Another menu begins with Chilled Cucumber & Yogurt Soup (page 46), followed by the chicken served with herbed tomatoes (page 64) and a bottle of dry Gewurztraminer.

California Ribs

Combine water, vinegar, soy sauce, sugar, garlic, onions, oil, ginger, honey and Tabasco in a large bowl. Stir well to combine.

Arrange beef strips in a shallow glass or ceramic (non-metallic) roasting pan. Pour over marinade, cover, and refrigerate for 24 to 48 hours, turning ribs occasionally. (Longer marinating results in spicier ribs.)

Lift ribs from marinade (save marinade for other uses, if desired) and place on hot barbecue grill, positioned 4 to 6 inches above a solid bed of low-glowing coals. Cook for about 5 minutes per side for medium rare, turning ribs once until brown on both sides. Cut in serving-size portions and transfer to a large platter.

Makes 6 to 8 servings

Either beef or pork ribs are suitable for this recipe. Have your butcher start with a slab of ribs. Ask him to slice the ribs crosswise (across the bones) into long strips about ¾-inch wide. You can then cut these strips or "riblets" any length you desire. Try serving California Ribs with Fresh Tomato Tart (page 84). We think they are perfect for casual summer entertaining. The tangy marinade can also be used for barbecuing chicken or flank steak.

Marinade

3	*cups water*
1	*cup red wine vinegar*
1½	*cups soy sauce*
1	*cup sugar*
3	*tablespoons chopped garlic cloves*
3	*green onions (including some tops), sliced*
3	*tablespoons sesame oil*
2	*tablespoons minced fresh ginger*
1	*tablespoon honey*
2	*teaspoons Tabasco sauce*
4	*to 5 pounds beef ribs, cut crosswise into ¾-inch-wide strips (see directions below)*

Butterflied Lamb with Mustard

3½ pound leg of lamb, butterflied

1 cup wine-grained mustard, such as Dijon or Herbs de Provence

1 tablespoon soy sauce

2 tablespoons minced fresh ginger

1 tablespoon minced garlic

1 teaspoon fresh rosemary leaves (or ¼ teaspoon dried rosemary)

Trim any excess fat from the lamb as needed.

Combine mustard, soy sauce, ginger, garlic, and rosemary in a small bowl until blended. Rub mixture on both sides of the lamb until well coated. Cover and set aside for 4 hours (or refrigerate overnight).

To grill, lightly grease the barbecue grill with oil. Place meat on hot grill positioned 4 to 6 inches above a solid bed of low-glowing coals. Cook, turning once to brown both sides, for about 30 minutes (15 minutes per side). Brush occasionally with any remaining mustard baste.

Remove from grill, cover with foil to keep warm, and allow to stand for 5 minutes before cutting in thin, slanting slices to serve.

Makes about 6 servings

Special summertime accompaniments for this oudoor meal may include Jellied Gazpacho (page 44), any flavored rice and fresh steamed vegetables, plus a bottle of Pinot Noir or Cabernet. Either individual Fruit Tarts (page 71) or Fresh Fruit with Ice Cream & Crème Anglaise (page 70) are perfect choices for desserts.

Grilled Pork with Cilantro Butter

You can prepare the flavored butter and marinate the pork a day in advance, if desired.

Combine softened butter, cilantro, lime juice, parsley and white pepper to taste in a food processor. Whirl until smooth. (Or, combine ingredients thoroughly in a small bowl.) Place mixture on a sheet of waxed paper and roll up, shaping butter into a small log. Use the waxed paper to help with the rolling. Refrigerate for 4 to 8 hours or overnight. (Butter may be made and stored in freezer up to 2 weeks.)

Combine lime juice, lime peel, ginger, cilantro, and oil in a small bowl.

Pound butterflied pork with a heavy mallet until flattened evenly. With a small sharp knife, make 10 to 15 slits on both sides of the meat. Place pork in a shallow pan, pour over marinade, cover, and refrigerate turning meat occasionally, for 6 to 8 hours or overnight.

Remove meat from refrigerator and allow to come to room temperature. Lift from marinade (reserve marinade) and place on barbecue rack positioned 4 to 6 inches above a solid bed of glowing coals (or mesquite, see page 57). Grill for 10 to 15 minutes per side, turning once, or until meat thermometer inserted in thickest portion registers 150°. Brush with reserved marinade as meat cooks.

Transfer meat to cutting board, cover, and let stand for 5 minutes. Unwrap cilantro butter and cut into ¼-inch-thick slices. Cut meat in thin, slanting slices to serve, topped with rounds of flavored butter.

Makes 4 to 6 servings

Butter

½   cup (¼ lb.) butter, softened

3   tablespoons minced cilantro

3   tablespoons fresh lime juice

3   tablespoons minced parsley

    White pepper

Marinade

4   tablespoons fresh lime juice

1½   teaspoons grated lime peel

1   tablespoon finely minced ginger

¼   cup minced cilantro

½   cup olive oil

1   boneless pork loin (2 to 2½ lbs.), trimmed and butterflied

Taste the Seasons

Clockwise from right: frosty parfait glass of Strawberry Sorbet (page 69) served with Toffee Almond Cookies (page 68); Spinach-stuffed Chicken Breasts (page 58) accompanied by miniature zucchini and beets; Pasta Salad Niçoise (page 51); Minted Pea Soup (page 47).

Tomatoes—Two Methods

Herb Baked

7   *tablespoons butter*

½   *cup finely chopped onion*

1½   *teaspoons minced garlic*

¼   *cup chopped red pepper*

1   *tablespoon each minced parsley and basil*

4   *large tomatoes, cut in half crosswise and squeezed of juice*

     Salt and freshly ground pepper

2   *tablespoons all-purpose flour*

1   *cup half-and-half*

⅛   *teaspoon cayenne pepper*

Oven Dried

4   *firm ripe tomatoes*

     Vegetable spray

     Dried basil leaves (optional)

     Olive oil

To make herb baked tomatoes, preheat oven to 350°. Grease a shallow 9 × 13-inch baking dish with 1 tablespoon butter.

Melt 2 tablespoons butter in a frying pan. Add onions, garlic, and red pepper, and cook over medium heat for about 5 minutes. Add parsley and basil. Arrange tomatoes, cut-side-up, in prepared dish. Sprinkle with about 1 teaspoon salt and some pepper. Divide onion mixture and spoon over tops of tomatoes. Dot with 2 tablespoons butter. Bake for 20 to 25 minutes or until tender.

Meanwhile, melt remaining 2 tablespoons butter in a saucepan. Add flour and cook until bubbly. Slowly stir in half-and-half and cook until thickened. Season with salt and cayenne. Transfer tomatoes to a large platter and spoon some sauce over the top to serve. Offer remaining sauce separately.

To make oven-dried tomatoes, set oven to 200°. Spray two large baking sheets with vegetable spray.

Cut unpeeled tomatoes in half crosswise and squeeze out juice. Then cut each half into thirds. Arrange tomatoes in the pans, and sprinkle sparingly with basil leaves, if desired. (The more basil you use, the more intense the flavor will be after drying.)

Bake in the 200° oven for 8 to 10 hours or until tomatoes shrivel similar to dried apricots. Remove tomatoes in batches as they reach this stage. Cool completely and then pack into jars. Drizzle some olive oil over tomatoes, allowing a thin layer to rest on top. (This will prevent discoloration.) Store in the refrigerator for up to 3 weeks and use as indicated in recipes calling for sun-dried tomatoes. Makes 1½ to 2 cups.

Makes 8 servings

Eggplant Flan

Peel eggplant and cut into ½-inch-thick slices. Then cut slices into eighths and sprinkle with salt. Line a cookie sheet or jellyroll pan with paper towels. Arrange eggplant on toweling, cover with more towels, and then a second cookie sheet. Weight the top cookie sheet down with a few cans from the pantry. Set aside for 45 minutes to remove excess moisture from the eggplant.

Melt 2 tablespoons of the butter and 1 tablespoon oil in a very wide frying pan over medium heat. Add onions and sauté for 2 to 3 minutes. Add red pepper and cook for 5 to 7 minutes longer, stirring often. Add tomatoes and Italian herbs. Reduce heat and simmer, uncovered, for about 10 minutes or until liquid has evaporated. (Tomatoes will appear almost as a purée.)

Melt remaining 6 tablespoons butter and 1 tablespoon oil in a wide frying pan over medium heat. Add eggplant and sauté for 5 minutes until eggplant begins to turn brown. Cover, reduce heat, and simmer until all the liquid has evaporated. Season to taste with salt and pepper.

Preheat oven to 350°. Combine eggplant and tomato mixture and spoon into a 9-inch round cake pan or ovenproof dish. Whisk egg and cream together until smooth; add cayenne and season with salt and pepper. Spoon cream mixture over the vegetables, lifting them with a fork to allow cream to seep to the bottom of the baking dish.

Bake for about 20 minutes or until custard appears firm but still slightly creamy when tested with a knife.

Makes 6 servings

1 large eggplant (about 1½ lbs.)

Salt

½ cup (¼ lb.) butter

2 tablespoons olive oil

2 small onions, minced

1 red pepper, seeded and cut in julienne strips

1 pound tomatoes, peeled, seeded, and diced (or 14½ oz. can of Italian pear tomatoes)

½ teaspoon Italian herbs

Freshly ground pepper

1 lightly beaten egg

½ cup heavy cream

Pinch cayenne pepper

Focaccio

1 package active dry yeast

¼ cup warm water (about 110°)

½ teaspoon sugar

¾ cup warm water

6 to 8 tablespoons olive oil

3 cloves garlic, minced

1 teaspoon sugar

1 teaspoon salt

½ cup whole wheat flour

2½ to 3 cups unbleached flour

Topping

2 pounds white onions, very thinly sliced

2 tablespoons fresh thyme leaves, finely chopped (or 2 teaspoons dried)

Vegetable spray

Cornmeal

In a large bowl, sprinkle yeast over warm water and let stand for 5 minutes to soften. Stir in the ½ teaspoon sugar, and 1 tablespoon olive oil.

Combine the ¾ cup water, garlic, sugar, salt, and whole wheat flour. Add the yeast mixture, stirring to combine. Add the unbleached flour, ½ cup at a time, until a sticky dough is formed. (You should have about ½ cup flour left.)

Turn dough out onto a board dusted with remaining flour and knead for 10 to 12 minutes or until dough is smooth and elastic. Brush inside of a large bowl with oil, place dough inside, rotating it once to coat entire surface. Cover with plastic wrap and let rise in a warm place until doubled.

Meanwhile, place 2 or 3 tablespoons olive oil in each of two large frying pans. Cook half the onions in each pan over medium-low heat, stirring occasionally, for 30 minutes. Set pans aside.

Spray two cookie sheets with vegetable spray and dust with cornmeal. Punch down dough and divide in half. Knead each portion to form a ball and then roll each out into a 10-inch disc about ¼-inch thick. (Or, shape four 6-inch discs or eight 4-inch ones.) Transfer dough to prepared pans and brush top surface with oil that is left in the pans. Divide onions between rounds of dough, spreading them to within a ½-inch of the edge. Sprinkle with thyme. Cover and let rise for about 1 hour.

Preheat oven to 425°. Bake rounds in upper third of the oven for about 20 minutes or until golden brown. (Adjust baking time to about 15 minutes for smaller rounds.) Cut into wedges to serve, or serve whole if baked small.

Makes 10 to 12 servings

Greek Cookies

Cream butter and sugar together in a medium-size bowl until light and fluffy. Stir in egg yolk, lemon zest, and extract until combined.

Sift flour with baking powder into cream mixture, stirring until dough is well blended. Cover surface of dough with plastic wrap and refrigerate for at least 2 hours (or as long as 6 hours).

Preheat oven to 350°.

Remove half the dough from refrigerator; keep remaining dough chilled until ready to use. Divide and shape dough into ¾-inch-wide balls. Place three balls together in a triangle with edges touching on an ungreased cookie sheet. Press edges of balls together slightly. Repeat until cookie sheet is full.

Bake for 18 to 20 minutes. Remove and cool on a wire rack for 2 to 3 minutes. Dust with powdered sugar. Repeat procedure with remaining dough.

Makes 27 to 30 cookies

1   cup butter, softened

¼   cup sugar

1   egg yolk

2   teaspoons grated lemon zest

½   teaspoon anise extract

2   cups sifted all-purpose flour

1   teaspoon baking powder

    Powdered sugar

Simple-to-make Greek Cookies can be prepared ahead and frozen in an airtight container for up to 2 weeks. To serve, bring to room temperature and dust with additional powdered sugar, as needed. We think you'll agree that these gems have an outstanding flavor and pretty appearance.

Toffee Almond Cookies

1¾ cups all-purpose flour

¾ teaspoon baking powder

Pinch salt

2 tablespoons sugar

½ cup butter, softened

1 beaten egg

1 to 2 tablespoons heavy cream

Topping

½ cup heavy cream

1½ cups sugar

½ cup butter

½ cup honey

2 cups (6 oz.) sliced almonds

Preheat oven to 375°. Grease bottom of 10½ × 15-inch jellyroll pan with shortening.

Sift flour with baking powder and salt into a large bowl. Stir in sugar. Cut in butter with a pastry blender until crumbly; then add egg. Add cream, a little at a time, until mixture is moist enough to hold together.

Pat dough into prepared pan. Bake for 10 minutes and then remove; set aside.

Meanwhile, pour cream into a heavy, 2-quart saucepan. Add sugar, butter, and honey. Place over medium heat, stirring often with a wooden spoon, until butter melts and sugar dissolves. Insert a candy thermometer into mixture and then bring to a boil. Add almonds and continue boiling for about 15 minutes or until syrup thickens and registers 240° (soft-ball stage).

Remove thermometer and pour syrup evenly over baked cookie crust. Return to 375° oven for 15 to 18 minutes or until top is golden caramel color. Remove from oven to cool slightly. While still warm, cut into diamonds; then transfer cookies to a wire rack to cool completely. (Or cool, wrap tightly, and freeze up to 1 month.)

Makes 3 to 4 dozen

Unless you're experienced in candymaking or recognize the "soft-ball stage" readily, we recommend using a candy thermometer. And remember to cut the cookies while they're still warm. We enjoy serving these gems with refreshing strawberry sorbet as pictured on page 63.

Strawberry Sorbet with Grand Marnier

Process strawberries, orange juice, and lemon juice (in batches, if necessary) in a food processor or blender until smooth. Place in a large bowl and stir in sugar until well blended.

Spoon mixture into a shallow baking pan. Cover and freeze for about 3 hours or until almost firm.

Using food processor or blender, process half the mixture with 1 to 2 ounces liqueur until fluffy. Repeat with remaining mixture and liqueur. Return all sorbet to a shallow pan. Cover and freeze until firm. (For longer storage or for ease when serving, place sorbet in a deep, straight-sided plastic container fitted with a lid.)

Remove from freezer 10 to 15 minutes before serving. Scoop into chilled parfait glasses or other suitable stemware and garnish with a sprig of mint.

Makes 8 servings

3	baskets (12 oz.) strawberries, hulled
1½	cups fresh orange juice
½	cup lemon juice
2	cups sugar
2	to 4 ounces Grand Marnier
	Mint sprigs

For raspberry lovers, substitute 3 boxes of raspberries (10 oz. each) for 2 of the boxes of strawberries. Decrease the sugar to 1½ cups. You may want to force mixture through a strainer to remove the raspberry seeds. Do this just after blending the fruit and sugar together and before the first freezing. Serve with a special cookie such as Toffee Almond Cookies (left) as pictured on page 63.

Fresh Fruit with Ice Cream & Crème Anglaise

Crème Anglaise

2   *cups half-and-half*

3   *egg yolks*

½   *cup sugar*

1   *tablespoon Grand Marnier*

1   *quart vanilla ice cream*

3   *cups fresh fruit (sliced peaches, strawberries, or papaya, or whole berries)*

Heat half-and-half in a heavy saucepan until almost scalding. Remove from heat and set aside.

Meanwhile, whisk egg yolks and sugar together for 5 to 7 minutes or until mixture is pale in color and reaches the ribbon stage (mixture should form a trail of ribbon across its surface when the whisk is lifted).

Slowly, pour in some hot half-and-half and whisk to combine. Return entire mixture to remaining hot cream and stir until combined well. Place over low heat and cook, stirring constantly, until custard comes to a boil and thickens. Remove from heat and stir in the Grand Marnier; set aside to cool.

To serve, spoon about ¼ cup crème anglaise into the bottom of a round goblet. Add two small scoops of ice cream. Top with some fruit. Repeat for remaining servings.

Makes 8 servings

The fun of this versatile recipe is that you can use whatever fruit is available and ripe. You can also change the vanilla ice cream to another flavor as well—fresh apple or peach, any of the berry varieties, or even ones with nuts like toasted almond are all suitable substitutes.

Fruit Tarts

Prepare pastry dough as directed on page 35. (This may be done a day in advance.) Press into a 10 or 11-inch tart pan with a removable bottom and bake as directed. Remove from oven and cool.

Prepare pastry cream as directed on page 36 *except* substitute 1½ tablespoons Grand Marnier for the vanilla. (This may be done a day in advance.)

To assemble, brush bottom of baked pastry shell with half of the apricot preserves. Top with a ½-inch-thick layer of pastry cream. Peel kiwi and slice ⅛-inch thick; then cut slices in half.

Arrange kiwi slices in an overlapping pattern around edge of tart. Repeat with a smaller circle of slices inside. (You can overlap in the same direction, or reverse the direction of the slices for contrast.) Continue arranging slices until you have worked your way to the center. Place some raspberries (or blueberries) in the center for garnish.

Combine remaining warm preserves with remaining Grand Marnier. Using a pastry brush, glaze the top of the tart until well coated.

Cut in wedges to serve.

Makes 8 to 10 servings

You can substitute 8 cups raspberries, blueberries, sliced peaches, or any combination of the above for the kiwi. For dark colored fruit, use red currant jelly instead of apricot preserves and mound the berries attractively over the pastry cream. Six small 4-inch tarts can be made using about 1 cup fruit each, as pictured on page 11.

Dough

1   recipe Dough (page 35)

Filling

1   recipe Pastry Cream (page 36, with substitution noted at left)

1   jar (13 oz.) apricot jam, strained and warmed

3   tablespoons Grand Marnier

8   kiwi fruit

     Raspberries (or blueberries), for garnish

Apple & Berry Cobbler

3   medium tart apples, peeled and sliced

2   boxes (8 oz. each) blackberries, rinsed

8   tablespoons sugar

Dough

1½   cups all-purpose flour

1   teaspoon baking powder

1½   teaspoons salt

¼   cup lard (or shortening)

¼   cup butter

½   cup heavy cream

¼   cup melted butter

1   cup heavy cream

Generously butter a shallow, 2½-quart baking pan; set aside. Preheat oven to 425°.

Toss apple slices and berries together just to combine and spoon into prepared pan. Sprinkle fruit evenly with about 3 tablespoons sugar (if berries are tart, you may want to add a little more sugar).

Sift flour with baking powder and salt into a medium-size bowl. Add 3 tablespoons sugar. Using a pastry blender, cut in lard and butter until mixture reaches the consistency of cornmeal. Add the ½ cup cream, mix until a soft dough is formed.

Drop spoonfuls of dough over the fruit mixture and spread as well as possible with a rubber spatula. (Don't worry if the entire top isn't covered.) Brush melted butter over the top of the dough with a pastry brush and then sprinkle with remaining 2 tablespoons sugar.

Bake in preheated oven for 25 to 30 minutes or until top is puffy and lightly browned. Serve warm in small rimmed dishes with a pitcher of cream as the topping. (Or, whip the 1 cup heavy cream with a little sugar just until lightly beaten and offer alongside.)

Makes 6 to 8 servings

Let the availability of seasonal fruit suggest what kind of cobbler to serve. Sliced peaches, all types of berries, and combinations of 2 or more ripe fruits can be easily substituted. You'll need 6 to 7 cups of fruit for serving 6 to 8 guests.

Thoughts for Entertaining

Summer is a gentle time of lazy days and light-hearted evenings . . .

For a casual pool party, cover tables with beach towels. Decorate with brightly colored Chinese food boxes that have been weighted down and stuffed with tissue paper and silk or paper flowers. Festoon the garden with paper umbrellas or kites.

Use your garden's bounty to create a vegetable centerpiece. Place a few leafy-topped baby carrots in wine carafes filled with water, or pack various sizes of Mason jars with baby carrots, radishes, Japanese eggplants, and small zucchini.

For a western or southwestern theme, cover your table with denim or Mexican serapes and cluster clay pots filled with cacti in the center. Or, arrange varieties of yellow, green, and red peppers in a terra cotta saucer.

Plan a dinner offering each course in a different area of the house. Serve salad in the garden, dinner in the dining room, and dessert in the living room.

On the Fourth of July, line a replica of Uncle Sam's hat (or any straw hat) with plastic. Fill it with red zinnias, white daisies, and blue bachelor buttons. Let campaign posters and buttons complete the patriotic theme.

For festive poolside entertaining at dusk, center votive candles on rimmed plastic dinner plates. Circle the candles with flowers. Then launch the twinkling armada to float in the pool.

When buying paper goods for an informal mixer party, select a different color for each table. Alternate colors of plates in the buffet line and invite guests to sit at the table matching their plate.

Wagons and wheelbarrows make super outdoor servers.

AUTUMN

Clockwise: happy face of Autumn; antique basket combining dried and fresh flowers; wine picnic offering Tailgate Sandwich (page 86) and Tomato Tart (page 84) with assortment of wine and cheese; archway leading to Court of Abundance; fresco by Pedro de Lemos.

Autumn

Apricot Brie in Phyllo

1   small round (8 oz.) ripe Brie or Camembert

    Melted butter

⅓   cup apricot jam

4   sheets phyllo dough

    Slices of red and yellow apple

    Seedless grapes

    Small baguettes

Trim off any wax or peel from outside of Brie, leaving the edible rind intact. Butter a cookie sheet.

Brush some melted butter on top of Brie, then spread with apricot jam.

Brush each sheet of phyllo with melted butter and carefully stack one on top of each other in a pile. Trim stack of phyllo into a 13- or 14- inch square. Position round of Brie, jam-side-down, in the middle of the phyllo stack.

Fold over a 4-ply stack of sheets from one side to cover Brie. Next fold over the 4-ply stack from the opposite side. Repeat procedure with the remaining two sides until you have a "phyllo package". Brush entire surface of package with melted butter; then push corner edges inward to mold package into a round.

Place the package, seam-side-down, onto prepared baking sheet. Cover loosely with plastic wrap and place in freezer for 3 to 4 hours. (Or, place on a lightly buttered plate, cover with plastic and then with foil, and freeze up to 1 week.)

Preheat oven to 375°. Remove Brie from freezer and bake for 25 to 30 minutes or until phyllo turns golden brown.

Allow to stand a few minutes, then transfer to a serving plate. Set aside for about 5 minutes. Then garnish edge of platter with slices of apple, clusters of grapes, and sliced baguettes.

Makes 6 to 8 servings

For serving this appetizer to more than 8 guests, we recommend baking two small rounds rather than increasing the size of one round to over half a pound. Also, allow enough time for freezing the Brie—some testers experienced a slight oozing of cheese.

Six Onion Soup

Melt butter with oil in a large Dutch oven or 3-quart casserole. Add onions, leeks, green onions, garlic, and shallots, and cook over medium heat for 5 minutes, stirring occasionally. Sprinkle with sugar, salt, and pepper. Reduce heat and continue cooking, stirring often, for about 30 minutes or until onions are lightly browned and reduced in bulk by half.

Stir in flour and cook for 1 minute. Slowly add beef stock until combined; then stir in sherry and thyme. Simmer, uncovered, stirring occasionally, for 10 minutes.

Meanwhile, preheat oven to 400°. Ladle soup into ovenproof bowls. Place a round of toasted bread on top and sprinkle generously with grated cheese. Make sure cheese covers the entire surface.

Place bowls on baking sheet in preheated oven for about 15 minutes or until cheese melts and turns golden brown.

Makes 8 servings

4	tablespoons butter
1	tablespoon olive oil
4	medium yellow onions, thinly sliced
3	white or Maui onions, thinly sliced
3	large leeks, rinsed, and sliced
4	green onions, thinly sliced
2	cloves garlic, minced
½	cup chopped shallots
¼	teaspoon sugar
1½	teaspoons salt
½	teaspoon pepper
2	tablespoons flour
6	cups beef stock
½	cup dry sherry
½	teaspoon dried thyme

Topping

8	rounds toasted French bread
½	pound grated Gruyère cheese

Almost a meal in itself when served with a hearty or coarse-textured bread and a bottle of Chenin Blanc.

Baked Mussel Soup with Cheese

6   dozen mussels, scrubbed and debearded

3   cups water

1   cup dry white wine

3   tablespoons butter

4   cups coarsely chopped onions

2   cloves garlic, minced

2   tablespoons all-purpose flour

3   tablespoons minced parsley

½   teaspoon crumbled dried thyme

    Salt and pepper

Topping

½   cup butter

6   slices French bread, cut ½-inch thick

¾   pound aged white Cheddar cheese, grated

Combine mussels, water, and wine in a large pan. Cover and steam over medium-high heat for 8 to 10 minutes until mussels open. (Discard any that don't open.) Ladle poaching liquid through a cheesecloth-lined strainer into a large measuring cup. Then add enough water to make 6 cups.

Remove mussels from shells, rinse, and set aside.

Melt the 3 tablespoons butter in a heavy, wide frying pan over medium heat. Add onions and garlic and cook, stirring frequently, until soft. Stir in flour and cook for about 3 minutes until bubbly. Slowly, add reserved liquid, whisking to combine until smooth. Add parsley, thyme, and salt and pepper to taste. Bring to a boil, reduce heat, and simmer for about 5 minutes.

Meanwhile, melt 3 tablespoons butter in a wide frying pan. Add 3 slices bread and brown on both sides over medium heat. Remove and repeat procedure with remaining butter and bread.

Preheat oven to 400°. Divide mussels and place in six ovenproof bowls. Ladle soup into each bowl and top with a piece of toasted bread. Cover bread with a liberal sprinkling of cheese and broil, 4 to 6 inches below element, for 2 minutes or until cheese browns.

Makes 6 servings

We think the perfect accompaniment for this delicious soup is a hearty salad and sourdough rolls. Don't cheat on the ingredients—the best ingredients will yield the best results so take care in selecting fresh mussels and a mild white Cheddar cheese.

Yam & Leek Soup

Trim off and discard root ends and tough green tops of leeks. Rinse thoroughly under running water to remove any dirt; then slice thinly.

Melt butter in a heavy Dutch oven or 3-quart pot over medium heat. Add leeks and yams and sauté for about 2 minutes, stirring often. Add chicken stock and mace.

Bring to a boil, cover, reduce heat, and simmer for 15 to 20 minutes or until tender. Cool slightly, then whirl in a blender or food processor, in batches if necessary, until smooth. (At this point, you can cover and refrigerate for up to 24 hours.)

Return soup to a saucepan and stir in half-and-half. Reheat just to serving temperature. Serve in individual soup bowls or earthenware tureen with a sprinkling of chives and bacon on top.

Makes 6 to 8 servings

1	*large bunch leeks*
4	*tablespoons butter*
2	*pounds yams, peeled and thinly sliced*
2	*cups chicken stock*
¼	*teaspoon ground mace*
3	*cups half-and-half*
	Snipped chives
	Crumbled, crisply-cooked bacon (optional)

Yams and leeks make a surprising, yet interesting flavor combination. Serve this simple-to-make soup with Cheese Braid (page 124) for a light, satisfying Sunday supper.

Parsnip & Spinach Soup

1   pound parsnips,
    trimmed, peeled and
    sliced

1   large onion, coarsely
    chopped

2   stalks celery
    (including leaves),
    sliced

4   cups chicken stock

½   pound spinach, stems
    removed

    Salt and freshly
    ground pepper

½   cup heavy cream

    Grated fresh nutmeg

Bring parsnips, onion, celery, and chicken stock to a boil over high heat. Cover, reduce heat, and simmer for about 25 minutes until parsnips are tender.

Cool slightly, then process in a blender or food processor in batches until smooth. With the last batch, add spinach leaves and process for 30 seconds.

Return purée to the pot and simmer for 2 to 3 minutes longer. Season to taste with salt and pepper. (At this point, you may cool, cover, and refrigerate up to 8 hours.)

Reheat soup to serving temperature and whisk in cream. (Avoid letting soup come to a boil as it might curdle.) Sprinkle individual servings with nutmeg.

Makes 6 servings

Following Parsnip & Spinach Soup, you might want to serve Fillets of Beef Provençal (page 89) with a Zinfandel wine. We suggest Poached Pears in Custard & Chocolate (page 102) or Marzipan Torte (page 104) for dessert.

Sausage & Lentil Soup

Rinse lentils, drain, and then soak in enough water to cover for 4 to 6 hours (or overnight). Drain and set aside.

Cut bacon into small pieces and cook in a heavy stock pot or 6-quart casserole until limp. Add onion, celery, carrots, and garlic; cook over medium heat for 3 to 4 minutes. Stir in potatoes, tomato paste, lentils, bay leaves, water, beef stock, salt, and pepper. Cover, reduce heat, and simmer for 1 to 1½ hours or until lentils are soft.

Stir in vinegar. Crumble sausages and add to soup. Then stir in leeks, cover, and simmer for 15 minutes more. Adjust seasonings with salt and pepper, as needed.

Makes 8 to 10 servings

We found that the flavor of this hearty soup intensifies if made at least a day before serving. Once stored in refrigerator, any excess fat may be skimmed off before reheating. And since it freezes well, why not double the recipe and freeze some for future use? We like serving this soup with homemade rye bread and cold beer.

1	*package (16 oz.) dried lentils*
5	*strips bacon*
1	*large onion, chopped*
2	*cups celery, thinly sliced*
1	*cup carrots, thinly sliced*
2	*cloves garlic, minced*
2	*cups diced potatoes*
½	*cup tomato paste*
2	*bay leaves*
6	*cups water*
4	*cups beef stock*
2½	*teaspoons salt*
½	*teaspoon pepper*
2	*tablespoons red wine vinegar*
2	*spicy hot Italian sausages, casings removed*
4	*mild Italian sausages, casings removed*
3	*large leeks, trimmed, rinsed and sliced*

Greek Country Salad

Dressing

4 tablespoons red wine vinegar

½ teaspoon salt

¾ teaspoon dried oregano

Freshly ground pepper

⅔ cup olive oil

1 small head curly endive

1 head red leaf lettuce

2 cucumbers, peeled and sliced

12 to 16 cherry tomatoes, halved

3 green onions (including some tops), thinly sliced

2 tablespoons capers

¼ pound feta cheese, crumbled

Anchovy fillets

Greek olives

Sprigs of parsley

Combine vinegar, salt, oregano, and pepper in a small bowl. Slowly whisk in oil until well blended. Cover and refrigerate, if made ahead.

Tear endive and red lettuce into bite-size pieces and place in a large salad bowl. Add cucumbers, tomatoes, green onions, capers, and feta cheese. Toss lightly to combine. Whisk dressing to blend, pour over salad, and toss.

Arrange portions on individual salad plates. Garnish each with an anchovy fillet, a few olives, and a sprig of parsley.

Makes 6 to 8 servings

Eggplant Salad with Fontina & Pesto

Slice, but don't peel, eggplant into ½-inch-thick rounds. Sprinkle both sides with salt and place rounds on paper towels for about 45 minutes.

Meanwhile, combine garlic, basil, cheese, vinegar, and oil in a blender or food processor and whirl until smooth. Season to taste with salt and pepper; cover and set aside.

Pat any excess moisture from eggplant slices. Arrange in single layers on two large baking sheets. Preheat broiler.

Lightly brush both sides of eggplant with olive oil. Place baking sheets 2 to 4 inches below broiler element and cook, turning slices once, until lightly browned. (You may need to do this in batches.)

Remove, cool slightly, and cut into large pieces. Place in a bowl and add fontina, onions, green pepper, red pepper, and dressing. Toss gently to combine and serve on a bed of lettuce.

Makes 4 to 6 servings

This eggplant salad with its pesto-flavored dressing and cubes of fontina cheese is appealing to those who are especially fond of eggplant, although many testers found that even though they didn't think they liked eggplant, they enjoyed this interesting salad. It's perfect as a side dish for barbecued hamburgers or other grilled meats.

2	*medium eggplants (about 2½ lbs. total)*
	Salt and freshly ground pepper

Dressing

1	*large clove garlic*
½	*cup firmly packed basil leaves*
¼	*cup grated Parmesan cheese*
2	*tablespoons white wine vinegar*
⅓	*cup olive oil*
	Salt and freshly ground pepper
	Olive oil
8	*ounces fontina cheese, cut in small cubes*
6	*green onions, diagonally sliced*
1	*large green pepper, seeded and diced*
1	*cup roasted sweet red pepper, cut in thin julienne strips*
	Lettuce

Fresh Tomato Tart

Dough

1   recipe Dough (page 35, with substitution noted at right)

Filling

2   tablespoons olive oil

3   pounds tomatoes, peeled, seeded, and chopped

½   cup chopped onions

2   cloves garlic, minced

1   lightly beaten egg

4   egg yolks

½   teaspoon each dried oregano, thyme, and salt

8   anchovies, chopped

4   tablespoons each tomato paste and chopped parsley

3   zucchini, sliced

Thin tomato slices

Olive oil

About ¼ cup grated Parmesan cheese

Prepare dough as directed on page 35 but eliminate the sugar. Roll out on a floured board to a thickness of ⅛-inch. Fit into an 11-inch tart pan. Return to refrigerator while making filling.

Heat oil in a wide frying pan over medium heat. Add tomatoes, onions, and garlic and cook, stirring occasionally, for about 3 minutes until soft. Increase heat and cook for 5 minutes or until liquid is almost evaporated. Cool slightly. Preheat oven to 400°.

Whisk egg and egg yolks together in a bowl. Add oregano, thyme, salt, anchovies, tomato paste, and parsley. Combine egg mixture with tomato mixture; set aside.

Bake pastry shell in preheated oven for about 15 minutes. Remove from oven and reduce temperature to 375°. Pour filling into pastry shell. Cover surface with slices of zucchini. Arrange enough overlapping slices of tomato to cover the top and brush with some olive oil. Sprinkle with about ¼ cup cheese and return to oven for 30 minutes or until top is lightly browned.

Makes 8 to 10 servings

Serve this flavorful tart at room temperature as an accompaniment to simply grilled chicken or meat. Or, offer wedges to guests at a tailgate party, picnic, or wine tasting such as the one pictured on pages 74 and 75.

Spaghetti with Scallops, Mussels & Shrimp

Heat oil in a wide frying pan over low heat. Add garlic and cook, stirring occasionally, for 2 to 3 minutes until garlic just begins to turn brown. Remove and discard garlic. Stir in salt, pepper, basil, and oregano. (Avoid letting herbs brown.) Add tomatoes and stir to combine. Simmer, uncovered, for 20 to 30 minutes, stirring occasionally. Remove from heat and stir in parsley and anchovy paste. (This may be done in advance and refrigerated up to 1 day.)

Cook spaghetti in boiling salted water until *al dente* (still slightly firm to the bite).

Meanwhile, reheat sauce to simmering if made ahead. Add mussels, cover, and cook for 5 minutes until shells open half way. Add scallops and shrimp, cover and simmer for 2 to 3 minutes longer or until shrimp begin to turn pink.

Drain spaghetti well and place some on each dinner plate. Spoon some sauce and some of each shellfish over spaghetti. Sprinkle with grated cheese and offer additional cheese at the table.

Makes 4 servings

Before you're tempted to use canned marinara sauce, try this recipe—it's quick and easy and has such a wonderful flavor you may want to double the recipe and freeze the rest. Pictured on page 94, we think our pasta and shellfish dish goes well with crusty sourdough rolls, a salad of mixed greens, and a bottle of Merlot or Barbera.

Sauce

¼	cup olive oil
3	large cloves garlic
1½	teaspoons salt
½	teaspoon freshly ground pepper
2	teaspoons dried basil
2	teaspoons dried oregano
1½	pounds tomatoes, peeled, seeded and chopped
3	tablespoons minced parsley
1	tablespoon anchovy paste
¾	pound spaghetti
1¼	pounds mussels, scrubbed and debearded
1	pound scallops, halved
¾	pound large shrimp, peeled and deveined
	Grated Parmesan cheese

Tailgate Sandwich

Relish

1½   cups chopped pimiento-stuffed olives

1   cup chopped ripe olives

2   tablespoons capers, drained

3   or 4 anchovies, chopped

⅔   cup olive oil

1½   tablespoons lemon juice

⅓   cup minced parsley

2   cloves garlic, minced

1   teaspoon dried oregano

8-inch round loaf of French bread

⅔   pound mortadella, thinly sliced

⅔   pound provolone or jack cheese, thinly sliced

⅔   pound Italian salami, thinly sliced

Combine olives, capers, anchovies, olive oil, lemon juice, parsley, garlic, and oregano in a small bowl. Cover and chill for 2 to 4 hours or for as long as 2 days.

To assemble sandwich, split loaf of bread in half horizontally. Remove some of the soft inside bread from both top and bottom, leaving about a ¾-inch-thick shell.

Brush inside of top and bottom shells with excess marinade from bottom of relish bowl. Stir relish to blend and then spoon half onto bottom round of bread. Arrange all the mortadella slices over relish. Then layer provolone slices, followed by salami.

Mound remaining relish over that and cover with top shell. Wrap entire sandwich tightly with plastic wrap and position a 5-pound weight on top. (Placing the loaf in a round cake pan and resting an ordinary brick on top works nicely!) Chill for 1 hour.

Cut sandwich into wedges with a long serrated knife and serve.

Makes 6 to 8 servings

For a large crowd, have a local bakery make a 10-inch loaf of bread for you. Increase the meats and cheese to 1 pound each and the relish ingredients by a third. We suggest Cabernet or Pinot Noir as a suitable wine. Tailgate Sandwich may be prepared a day before serving. It is pictured at our wine tasting picnic on pages 74 and 75.

Sole Vin Blanc

Wipe fish with a damp cloth and set aside.

Melt butter in a wide frying pan over medium heat. Stir in onion and parsley, cooking for about 2 minutes until softened. Arrange fish fillets over onion-parsley mixture and sprinkle with salt and pepper. Pour wine and lemon juice around, but not directly over, the fish. Cover, reduce heat, and simmer for 3 to 4 minutes.

Carefully lift out fish and transfer to warm dinner plates; keep warm.

Bring reserved wine mixture to a boil and cook for 1 to 2 minutes or until reduced to about ¼ cup. Whisk in cream and heat for 1 to 2 minutes longer or until slightly thickened.

Spoon sauce over fish and garnish edges of plate with parsley springs and lemon twists.

Makes 4 servings

4	sole fillets (about 6 oz. each), such as petrale or Dover
2	tablespoons butter
¼	cup minced onion
1	tablespoon minced parsley
	Salt and white pepper
½	cup dry white wine
1½	tablespoons lemon juice
½	cup heavy cream
	Sprigs of parsley
	Thin slices of lemon

Fast and quite simple to prepare, this popular sole recipe with its delicate lemon-cream sauce received raves from our busy testers. Glazed carrots (page 29), an herb-flavored rice, and dry Riesling or Gewurztraminer make excellent accompaniments.

Tostada Soup with Fresh Salsa

3   pounds beef stew, trimmed and cut into small pieces

3   cups beef stock

2   large onions, thinly sliced

1   medium red pepper, seeded and chopped

1   can (4 oz.) diced chiles, drained

1   can (28 oz.) tomatoes and their juice

1½   cups corn

1   tablespoon jalapeño salsa

     Salt and freshly ground pepper

Garnish

½   head shredded iceberg lettuce

1½   cups shredded Cheddar cheese

     Chopped tomatoes

     Sour cream

     Sliced avocado

     Tortilla chips

Prepare salsa (see recipe below) as directed. Cover and refrigerate for 4 hours or overnight. Drain off excess liquid before serving.

In a large Dutch oven or stockpot, combine beef, beef stock, onions, red pepper, and chiles. Bring to a boil, cover, reduce heat, and simmer for 1½ hours. Stir in tomatoes, cover, and simmer for 1 hour longer or until meat is tender.

Add corn and jalapeño salsa; season to taste with salt and pepper. Simmer, uncovered, for about 5 minutes.

Arrange separate bowls of each garnish, or place items separately on a large platter. Ladle soup into individual bowls, tuck a few tortilla chips around the edges, and top with fresh salsa and your choice of garnishes.

Makes 8 to 10 servings

Delicious, simple-to-make, and fun to serve were the comments we often heard from our testers about Tostada Soup. To make fresh salsa, combine 3 finely chopped tomatoes, ¾ cup chopped green onion, 3 tablespoons chopped green chiles, ½ teaspoon ground coriander, and salt and pepper to taste. Crusty bread or steamed flour tortillas and a glass of Mexican beer make excellent accompaniments.

Fillets of Beef Provençal

Melt butter in a wide frying pan over low heat. Add onion and pepper and cook, stirring occasionally, for 3 to 5 minutes until all the moisture has evaporated. Stir in tomatoes, increase heat to high, and cook until all juice has evaporated. Add sugar and savory and season to taste with salt and pepper. Keep warm or prepare up to 2 to 4 hours in advance and reheat just before serving.

Place a heavy, wide frying pan over medium-high heat. Sprinkle surface with salt. Add beef fillets and sauté, turning once to brown both sides, for about 4 minutes per side for rare.

Reduce heat to medium. Then pour in warm brandy and ignite. When flames die down, lift out fillets and transfer to a warm serving platter (reserving pan for making sauce).

To the pan, add butter and melt over medium heat. Stir in flour and cook for 1 minute. Add tomato paste, garlic, wine, beef stock, and Worcestershire. Increase heat and boil rapidly for 1 minute.

Spoon sauce over each fillet and top with some vegetable garnish to serve.

Makes 6 servings

With or without the vegetable garnish, you'll enjoy serving this easy version of pan-fried steak with your choice of vegetable purée (page 96) and buttered small new potatoes. For dessert, we suggest Poached Pears in Custard & Chocolate (page 102).

Garnish

4	tablespoons butter
1	large yellow onion, very finely chopped
1	large green pepper, seeded and minced
3	tomatoes, seeded and finely chopped
½	teaspoon each sugar and savory
	Salt and freshly ground pepper
6	beef fillets
	Salt
3	tablespoons warm brandy

Sauce

3	tablespoons butter
1	tablespoon flour
1½	tablespoons tomato paste
1	clove garlic, minced
1	cup dry red wine
½	cup beef stock
1	teaspoon Worcestershire

Corned Beef Bake

Glaze

¼ cup honey

¼ cup spicy brown mustard

¼ cup brown sugar

3 to 3½-pound corned beef brisket, without added spices (suitable for baking)

Combine honey, mustard, and brown sugar in a small bowl until blended.

Trim any excess fat from all sides of beef brisket, if necessary. Heavily coat all sides of the brisket with glaze and place in a roasting pan.

Cover loosely with foil and bake in a 300° oven for about 3 hours or until tender. Remove foil during the last 30 minutes of baking and baste meat occasionally with pan juices to keep moist.

Remove and set aside for 5 minutes; then cut across the grain in thin slices to serve.

Makes 4 to 6 servings

This easy corned beef recipe is delicious—its flavor is guaranteed to please the entire family. Serve it hot with seasonal vegetables and boiled new potatoes, or warm, or at room temperature in hearty sandwiches. Our testers found that corned beef brisket comes many ways. Check the package to be sure it specifies the meat is "suitable for baking" rather than for boiling. Many butchers carry corned beef brisket, too; be sure to ask if it's for baking as a butcher will often carry both types.

Roast Duckling with Mixed Fruit

Combine mixed dried fruit, bourbon, and orange juice in a medium bowl. Cover and set aside to soak for at least 4 hours.

Meanwhile, melt butter in a large frying pan over medium-high heat. Add celery, onion, and apple and sauté for about 8 minutes, stirring occasionally, until tender. Add cinnamon, ginger, and nuts.

Combine fruit and vegetable mixtures in a large pan or covered casserole. Cover and simmer over low heat for about 15 minutes. Add more orange juice, as needed, if fruit becomes too dry. (This may be done up to 2 days in advance; reheat to serving temperature to serve.)

Meanwhile, preheat oven to 425°. Remove all excess fat from under the skin and from underside of duck. Season with salt and pepper. Place duck on a rack in a roasting pan. Cook for about 1 hour; then remove from oven and pour off excess fat. Reduce oven temperature to 350° and return duck to roast for 20 to 30 minutes longer or until skin is brown and crisp and temperature reaches 165° to 170°. Remove duck, cover loosely with foil and keep warm.

Pour off fat from pan. Deglaze pan with ½ cup orange juice and ¼ cup water; then prepare a gravy with remaining pan juices.

Spoon fruit dressing on to a serving platter. Place duckling on top and offer gravy separately to serve.

Makes 4 servings

You can split the duckling in half or cut in quarters before roasting, if desired. Duck halves or quarters take approximately 55 to 65 minutes when roasted the entire time in a 425° oven.

12	*ounces dried mixed fruit, diced*
¼	*cup bourbon*
1	*cup fresh orange juice*
2	*tablespoons butter*
1	*stalk celery, diced*
1	*large onion, diced*
1	*large tart apple, diced*
½	*teaspoon ground cinnamon*
½	*teaspoon ground ginger*
½	*cup coarsely chopped macadamia nuts*
½	*cup chopped pecans*
1	*duckling (5 to 6 lbs.)*
	Salt and freshly ground pepper
½	*cup orange juice*
¼	*cup water*

Sausage-stuffed Pork with Mustard Sauce & Vegetables

1   center-cut pork loin
     roast (3 to 3½
     lbs.), boned and tied

     Salt and freshly
     ground pepper

Stuffing

1   lightly beaten egg

½   pound lightly
     seasoned pork
     sausage

¼   cup finely chopped
     onion

2   tablespoons minced
     parsley

2   packages frozen
     spinach, thawed and
     squeezed of excess
     moisture

Vegetables

1   pound green beans,
     trimmed and cut in
     3-inch lengths

1   pound carrots,
     peeled and cut in
     3-inch julienne
     strips

4   medium yellow
     squash, cut in
     3-inch julienne strips

Unroll roast and place on a flat work surface. Sprinkle the inside with salt and pepper; set aside.

To make stuffing, combine egg, pork sausage, onion, parsley, and spinach until well blended. Spread stuffing evenly over inside of roast. Roll up roast and secure by tying in many places with kitchen string.

Place meat in a roasting pan and bake in a 350° oven for about 1½ hours or until temperature registers 175° on a meat thermometer. (Calculate about 30 minutes per pound for cooking time and weigh roast after it has been stuffed.)

Arrange beans and carrots in two small bundles on a large steaming rack. Place over boiling water, cover, and steam for about 5 minutes. Arrange squash in a bundle and place on steaming rack near other vegetables. Cover and steam for 5 minutes more or until carrots are just tender crisp. Keep warm.

Remove meat from oven, cover loosely with foil, and set aside while making sauce and finishing vegetables.

To make sauce, melt butter in a medium saucepan over medium heat. Add flour and cook, stirring often, for about 1 minute. Stir in chicken stock, ½ cup at a time, and whisk until smooth. Add beef bouillon and cook, stirring often, until sauce comes to a boil and thickens. Remove from heat and whisk in mustard, salt, and pepper; keep warm.

Heat butter with dill, salt, and pepper; keep warm.

Slice meat ½-inch thick and arrange in overlapping slices down the center of a large, warm serving platter. Arrange some of the vegetables, in bundles, at each corner of the platter; spoon some dill butter over each. Offer remaining vegetables and dill butter separately at the table.

Makes 6 to 8 servings

⅓	cup butter
3	sprigs fresh dill, minced
1	teaspoon salt
	Freshly ground pepper

Sauce

3	tablespoons butter
3	tablespoons all-purpose flour
2½	cups chicken stock
⅓	cup beef bouillon (consommé)
3	tablespoons spicy brown mustard
¼	teaspoon salt
1	teaspoon white pepper (or coarsely ground pepper)

We also enjoy serving Brussels sprouts or cabbage wedges with hearty entrées such as this, but you can substitute steamed carrots or Vegetable Purée (page 96) instead. A full-bodied Zinfandel or Cabernet is our choice for a complimenting wine.

Taste the Seasons

Clockwise from right: fireside table setting features unusual collection of Oriental objects; Persimmon Pudding (page 101) baked in tin molds cools on windowsill; impressive entrée, Spaghetti with Scallops, Mussels & Shrimp (page 85).

Vegetable Purée

Carrot-Squash

1½ pounds banana
    squash (in 1 piece)

4   large carrots

2   tablespoons heavy
    cream

2   tablespoons sour
    cream

2   tablespoons unsalted
    butter

¼   teaspoon curry
    powder

¼   teaspoon ground
    ginger

    Salt and freshly
    ground pepper

Broccoli

3   pounds broccoli,
    trimmed

3   tablespoons sour
    cream
4
    tablespoons grated
    Parmesan cheese
2
    tablespoons melted
    butter

    Salt and freshly
    ground pepper

    Ground nutmeg

To make carrot-squash purée, place squash, rind-side-up, in a steamer positioned over boiling water. Cover and steam for 20 to 30 minutes or until soft.

Meanwhile, peel and slice enough carrots to make 4 cups. Cook in boiling water for 10 to 12 minutes until tender; drain and set aside.

Scrape pulp from squash and place in a food processor. Add carrots and process until smooth and puréed. Add cream, sour cream, butter, curry powder, and ginger. Process until well blended. Season to taste with salt and pepper.

Place in a shallow baking dish, cover loosely with foil, and bake in a 350° oven for about 25 minutes or until heated through.

To make broccoli purée, cut off flowerets (reserve stalk for other uses). Place in boiling water and cook for about 5 minutes or until tender. Plunge into cold water to stop the cooking process; drain well.

Transfer broccoli to a food processor and whirl until puréed. (You should have about 3 cups.) Add sour cream, Parmesan cheese, and melted butter; process until well blended. Season to taste with salt, pepper and ground nutmeg.

Place in a shallow baking dish, cover loosely with foil, and bake in a 350° oven for about 25 minutes or until heated through.

Makes 6 servings

Cauliflower with Chiles & Cheese

Core cauliflower and break into small flowerets. Steam over boiling water for 4 to 5 minutes until just tender crisp. Drain well and then combine with 2 tablespoons butter.

Stir in chiles, onion, cheese, sour cream, salt and pepper. Spoon mixture into a shallow 2-quart baking dish. Sprinkle with bread crumbs and dot with remaining butter.

Bake in 350° oven for 25 to 30 minutes or until top is lightly browned.

Makes 6 servings

1	medium head cauliflower
4	tablespoons butter
1	can (4 oz.) chopped green chiles, drained
½	cup minced green onion (including some tops)
1½	cups grated Cheddar cheese
1	cup sour cream
1	teaspoon salt
¼	teaspoon freshly ground pepper
¾	cup dry bread crumbs

Even those who don't like cauliflower love this! We consider it suitable for a vegetarian entrée or as an accompaniment with any simple meat or chicken dish. This recipe can be prepared in advance. Reserve the bread crumbs until just before baking.

Cranberry Nut Loaves

2   cups (1 lb.) fresh cranberries, rinsed

1   cup all-purpose flour

1   cup unprocessed bran

2   teaspoons baking powder

½   teaspoon baking soda

1   cup sugar

1   lightly beaten egg

2   tablespoons melted butter

¾   cup orange juice

1   tablespoon grated orange zest

1   cup chopped walnuts

You'll need a sharp knife to cut—not coarsely chop—each cranberry in half. (Yes, testing has proven that slicing each berry in two *does* make a difference, both in texture and in the taste of the finished loaf.) Place halved cranberries in a small bowl; set aside.

Preheat oven to 350°. Grease bottoms of three 2 × 5 × 3½-inch loaf pans with shortening.

Combine flour, bran, baking powder, baking soda, and sugar in a large bowl. Stir in egg, butter, orange juice, and zest until blended. Fold in cranberries and walnuts. Divide evenly among prepared pans.

Bake for 45 to 50 minutes or until toothpick inserted in center comes out clean. Cool for 10 minutes, remove loaves from pans, and set aside on rack to cool completely.

Makes 3 loaves

Perfect for holiday gift giving, these flavorful loaves of bread can be baked ahead and then frozen up to 2 months. Use the small foil loaf pans, available at most markets, to simplify baking. Once cool, return loaves to original pans, then store, or even gift wrap.

Fresh Pear Coffeecake

Preheat oven to 350°. Lightly grease a 9-inch square baking pan with shortening.

Sift flour with cinnamon, nutmeg, and salt into a large bowl. Stir in sugar. Cut in butter with a pastry blender until mixture resembles cornmeal.

Sprinkle half the mixture into prepared pan and press in, but *very* lightly. Peel pears and cut into large chunks (at least 1-inch squares), distributing them evenly over sugar-flour mixture.

Stir baking soda into sour cream and pour into reserved sugar-flour mixture. Add egg and stir until well blended. Pour batter evenly over pears and sprinkle surface with pecans.

Bake for 40 to 50 minutes or until top is lightly browned and cake pulls away from sides of pan.

Makes 6 to 9 servings

2	cups all-purpose flour
1	teaspoon ground cinnamon
½	teaspoon ground nutmeg
¼	teaspoon salt
2	cups firmly packed brown sugar
½	cup butter, softened
2	large Bartlett pears
1	teaspoon baking soda
1	cup sour cream
1	lightly beaten egg
½	cup chopped pecans

Using good-size chunks of pears makes a big difference, according to our testers. The result is a delicious, easy-to-prepare coffeecake that can be served warm from the oven for Sunday brunch, or when time is at a premium and you want a freshly baked coffeecake in less than an hour.

The Ultimate Cookie

1	cup butter
1	cup sugar
1	cup packed brown sugar
1	lightly beaten egg
1	cup salad oil
2	teaspoons vanilla
1	cup crushed cornflakes (or other multi-grain cereal flakes)
3½	cups sifted all-purpose flour
1	teaspoon baking soda
½	teaspoon salt
1	cup old-fashioned rolled oats
½	cup flaked coconut
½	cup chopped pecans
½	cup chopped macadamia nuts
1	cup chocolate chips (or half chocolate chips and half raisins)

Preheat oven to 325°.

Cream butter and sugars together until smooth. Stir in egg, oil, and vanilla until blended. Add cornflakes and stir until combined.

Sift flour with baking soda and salt into the butter-sugar mixture and stir to combine. Add oats, coconut, pecans, macadamia nuts, and chocolate chips. Stir until all ingredients are combined well.

Using a large tablespoon of dough for each cookie, place spoonfuls onto an ungreased cookie sheet about 2 inches apart. Flatten top slightly with a fork. (You'll probably get 9 to 12 cookies on each sheet.)

Bake for 10 to 12 minutes or until lightly brown. Remove and let stand for several minutes, then transfer to a wire rack to cool completely.

Makes about 4 dozen

One of the best all-around cookies we've tasted. We think the addition of macadamia nuts pleases adult tastes. Expect this recipe to become one of your family's favorites.

Persimmon Pudding with Lemon Sauce

Grease a 2-quart pudding mold and its lid with shortening. (You can substitute foil for the lid.)

Peel persimmons and pull (or cut off) the flesh and place it in a blender or food processor. Whirl until smooth, then transfer to a measuring cup. You should have about 1 cup purée. Stir in baking soda; set aside.

Cream butter with sugar in a large bowl until fluffy. Add eggs, vanilla, lemon juice, brandy, and persimmon purée, whisking well to combine. Sift flour with cinnamon and salt into persimmon mixture. Stir to combine; fold in raisins and walnuts.

Spoon mixture into prepared mold and secure lid (or cover tightly with foil). Place on a rack in a large pot filled with 2 inches of boiling water. Cover and steam for 2½ hours, adding more boiling water as needed.

Remove and set aside for 10 minutes to cool. To make sauce, combine sugar, cornstarch, water, and orange juice in a small saucepan over medium heat. Cook, stirring often, for 3 to 4 minutes until thickened. Reduce heat and simmer for 1 to 2 minutes longer or until sauce is transparent. Stir in zest, lemon juice, and butter. Cool.

Invert pudding onto serving plate to unmold. Offer lemon sauce separately.

Makes 10 servings

3	medium very ripe persimmons
1½	teaspoons baking soda
½	cup butter, softened
1½	cups sugar
2	lightly beaten eggs
1½	teaspoons vanilla
1	teaspoon lemon juice
1	tablespoon brandy
1	cup flour
1¼	teaspoons cinnamon
¼	teaspoon salt
1	cup raisins
½	cup chopped walnuts

Sauce

⅓	cup sugar
1½	teaspoons cornstarch
⅔	cup water
⅔	cup orange juice
2	teaspoons grated lemon zest
2	tablespoons fresh lemon juice
2	tablespoons butter

The ideal autumn dessert—steamed persimmon pudding studded with raisins and walnuts as shown on page 94, topped with a fresh tangy lemon sauce.

Poached Pears in Custard & Chocolate

Custard

2	*lightly beaten eggs*
1⅓	*cups milk*
¼	*cup sugar*
2	*tablespoons Kahlua*
1	*teaspoon vanilla*
2½	*cups water*
½	*cup sugar*
2	*tablespoons lemon juice*
2	*cinnamon sticks*
3	*Bosc pears (6 oz. each)*

Sauce

4½	*to 5 ounces dark Swiss chocolate, broken in pieces*
¼	*cup heavy cream*
6	*Chocolate Leaves (page 40), for garnish*

Combine eggs, milk, and sugar in a blender or food processor until smooth. Transfer to a large wide frying pan and place over medium heat. Cook, whisking constantly, for about 4 minutes or until sauce thickens and coats the back side of a metal spoon. (Don't allow mixture to come to a boil.) Pour into a bowl and set aside to cool somewhat, then stir in Kahlua and vanilla. Cover and chill thoroughly. (Or, refrigerate up to 2 days.)

Combine water, sugar, lemon juice, and cinnamon in a large saucepan. Place over low heat and keep just below a boil.

Cut each pear in half. Carefully remove the center core section, taking care not to disengage the stem or bruise the pear. (It is easiest to leave a bit of the core attached at the top.) Using a sharp knife, score the skin of each pear in a decorative pattern. Flowing or curved lines that follow the shape of the pear look nice.

Arrange pear halves in hot syrup and poach for 5 minutes until tender. Remove, drain, and chill.

Melt chocolate in the top of a double boiler. Slowly whisk in cream until incorporated. Cover the bottom of 6 wide, shallow saucer-like dishes with custard. Lay a pear half, scored side up, in center of the pool of custard. (If pear appears moist, blot it first with a paper towel.)

Drizzle a ribbon of warm chocolate sauce in the custard forming a circle around pear at a point midway between pear and rim of the dish. Then, using a toothpick, pull (or swirl) through chocolate in several places to make a delicate, marbled design. Place a chocolate leaf near stem of pear for garnish.

Makes 6 servings

Hazelnut Meringue with Apricot Cream

Combine apricots (reserving 3 for garnish), sugar, lemon zest, and enough hot water to cover in a bowl. Set aside to soak for 1 hour.

Meanwhile, spread hazelnuts in a shallow pan and place in a 350° oven for 5 to 8 minutes, shaking pan occasionally, until lightly toasted. Cool completely, then whirl in a blender or food processor until cornmeal consistency. Transfer to a bowl and add 1 cup of the sugar.

Reduce oven to 325°. Lightly grease two 9-inch-round cake pans with shortening. Insert a 9-inch round of parchment in each. Lightly grease the parchment and dust with flour.

Using an electric mixer, beat egg whites until soft peaks form. With motor running, slowly add remaining 1½ cups sugar and cream of tartar; continue to beat until stiff peaks begin to form. Sprinkle nut-sugar mixture and vinegar over egg whites and fold together.

Spread meringue into prepared pans and bake for 40 to 45 minutes or until lightly browned. Cool slightly, then lift out meringue discs. Turn discs over and carefully peel off parchment; cool on a rack.

Meanwhile, drain liquid from apricots; whirl in a blender until puréed. Whip cream in a large bowl until stiff peaks form. Then fold in ¼ cup of the purée.

Place one layer of meringue on a serving plate and spread with half the apricot cream. Position top meringue layer so that edges align. Scoop remaining apricot cream into a pastry bag fitted with a No. 7 star tip. Pipe rosettes of cream over the top layer. Cut reserved apricots into thin slices. Garnish each rosette with a whole nut and a few slivers of apricot. Stir nectar and brandy into remaining purée until smooth and offer separately as a sauce.

Makes 8 servings

12	ounces dried apricots
2	tablespoons sugar
2	tablespoons lemon zest
	Hot water

Meringue

8	ounces hazelnuts (filberts)
2½	cups sugar
8	egg whites, room temperature
	Pinch cream of tartar
1	tablespoon vinegar
1	cup heavy cream
	Whole hazelnuts and slivers of dried apricot, for garnish
¾	cup (6 oz. can) apricot nectar
1	to 2 tablespoons apricot brandy

Marzipan Torte

Dough

1⅓	cups all-purpose flour
⅓	cup sugar
1	teaspoon baking powder
½	cup butter
1	lightly beaten egg
1	cup full-flavored raspberry preserves

Filling

½	cup butter, softened
⅔	cup sugar
1	cup almond paste, room temperature
½	teaspoon almond extract
2	lightly beaten eggs
¼	cup sliced almonds

Grease a 9-inch springform pan with butter. Preheat oven to 350°.

Combine flour, sugar, and baking powder in a large bowl. Using a pastry blender, cut in butter until mixture resembles cornmeal. Add the egg, mixing until dough is evenly moist and shapes into a ball. Flatten dough into a disc and press into bottom of prepared pan. Spread with ½ cup preserves. Cover and chill while preparing filling.

Cream butter and sugar together until fluffy. Break almond paste into small pieces and add gradually, blending a little after each addition. (This procedure can be done in a food processor.) Stir in extract and then eggs, one at a time, until mixture is well blended. Spoon filling evenly over chilled dough.

Bake for about 50 minutes or until lightly browned (center should still jiggle). Cool completely.

Meanwhile, spread almonds in a wide dry, frying pan and place over medium heat, shaking pan often, until toasted.

Release rim from springform pan. Spread remaining jam on top of torte and sprinkle with toasted almonds.

Makes 8 to 10 servings

The flavors of almond and raspberry blend together in this light, easy-to-prepare dessert. For chocolate lovers, we suggest spreading 6 ounces of melted semi-sweet chocolate on the cooling torte. When it hardens, spread with remaining jam and toasted almonds as directed.

Thoughts for Entertaining

Autumn is a spicy season, a glowing and abundant time of the year . . .

Design a fall arrangement using wheat, pumpkins, gourds, Indian corn, and other interesting foliage in a special basket or small wooden cart.

Plan a pasta party. Use a red-and-white checkered cloth for the table. Fill a basket with white and yellow mums and spike the arrangement with handfuls of uncooked spaghetti. Use wide lasagna noodles as placecards and insert them into crusty rolls. Even the napkins rings can be made of pasta. Soak 6-inch lengths of lasagna noodles in hot water until pliable. Bring ends together and overlap them slightly until a circle is formed. Press in between fingers a few minutes, then stand upright to dry.

Lacquer a dry loaf of braided bread with shellac or spray resin and adorn with dried autumn flowers, wheat, and ribbon.

Drape a beautiful *obi* down the center of your table. (Or try folding it in unusual ways.) Decorate the center of the table with a bonsai tree and a collection of small lacquer boxes or *netsukes* to complete the Oriental theme.

Think B I G ! Give a large scale party and serve oversized hamburgers with huge jars of mustard and pickles, and gigantic chocolate chip cookies. Use dish towels instead of napkins. Create a colossal centerpiece with pampas grass, corn stalks, and paper sunflowers.

Honor your favorite football team with a party. Cover the table with natural turf (sod). Place a football in the center of a ring mold filled with dense foliage. Accent the foliage with small pennants. Or line a helmet with plastic and fill it with flowers in your team's colors.

WINTER

Taste the Seasons

Clockwise: holiday unveiling of 20-foot Christmas tree laden with handmade and imported ornaments; fresh Dungeness crab (page 115); antique silver tray and cordial glasses from Traditional Shop's beautiful array of gifts; prolific orange tree in Court of Abundance.

Pancetta-wrapped Oysters

12 medium-size Pacific oysters, cleaned (reserve shells)

12 large fresh spinach leaves, stems removed

12 thin slices pancetta

Sauce

1 tablespoon butter

2 mushrooms, chopped

1 minced shallot

1 ounce Pernod

½ cup dry vermouth

2 tablespoons heavy cream

½ cup sweet butter, cut in chunks

Salt and freshly ground pepper

Select 12 of the best-looking oyster shell halves and set aside on a serving platter.

Wrap each oyster in a spinach leaf, covering the oyster completely. Then wrap each spinach bundle in a slice of pancetta, leaving the ends of the bundle exposed. Fasten with a toothpick (or thread them onto a pre-soaked wooden skewer).

Preheat broiler while making sauce.

Melt the 1 tablespoon butter in a wide frying pan over medium-high heat. Add mushrooms and shallot and sauté for 3 to 4 minutes. Whisk in Pernod and vermouth, scraping bottom of pan to deglaze. Add cream and cook, stirring often, until sauce is reduced by half. Remove from heat and whisk in butter, a few pieces at a time, stirring continuously as butter melts. Season to taste with salt and pepper.

Meanwhile, place oysters on broiling pan positioned 6 to 8 inches below element. Broil for about 3 minutes, then turn each over and broil 2 to 3 minutes longer.

Pour sauce through a strainer. Place one oyster in each shell and spoon a little sauce over top.

Makes 4 servings
You can buy oysters loose and serve them on small rimmed plates instead of using shells, if you prefer. Offer three oysters in a puddle of Pernod sauce to each guest as a first course with a sparkling wine. Pictured on page 126.

Scallop Mousseline with Lemon-Dill Sauce

Spray the inside of eight ½-cup mousseline molds or custard cups with vegetable spray. Set aside.

Whirl scallops and halibut together in a food processor or blender until finely chopped. Refrigerate for 30 minutes until cold without transferring from processor bowl.

Add eggs, salt, pepper, and nutmeg and whirl until combined. With motor running, slowly add cream; process for no more than 30 seconds.

Divide mixture and spoon into prepared molds. Place them in a deep baking dish filled with 1 inch warm water. Pierce a large sheet of foil with small holes (this allows steam to escape) and cover baking dish; wrap edges under to seal.

Bake in 350° oven for 30 minutes or until knife, inserted in center of mousseline, comes out clean.

Meanwhile, heat butter in a saucepan over medium heat. Add flour and cook, stirring often, for 1 to 2 minutes. Slowly add milk and continue to cook, stirring occasionally, until mixture comes to a boil. Whisk egg yolks and cream in a small bowl. Pour ½ cup hot sauce into egg-cream mixture, whisking continuously. Return to sauce and cook over medium heat until thick.

Remove from heat and stir in lemon juice, dill (or tarragon), sherry, and Worcestershire. Season to taste with salt and pepper.

To serve, invert each mousseline onto a small warm plate. Spoon some sauce over top and garnish with a tiny sprig of dill. Offer remaining sauce separately.

Makes 8 servings

½	pound bay scallops
¼	pound halibut, skinned and cut in pieces
3	lightly beaten eggs
½	teaspoon salt
¼	teaspoon white pepper
	Pinch nutmeg
2	cups heavy cream

Sauce

2	tablespoons butter
2	tablespoons flour
1½	cups milk
2	egg yolks
¼	cup heavy cream
1	tablespoon fresh lemon juice
2	teaspoons minced dill (or ¼ teaspoon dried tarragon)
1	tablespoon dry sherry
	Dash Worcestershire
	Sprigs of fresh dill

Gorgonzola Fettucine

8 ounces fresh fettucine

1 tablespoon oil

Sauce

¼ cup butter

1 egg yolk

⅓ cup milk

¼ cup heavy cream

4 ounces Gorgonzola, crumbled

Freshly ground pepper

⅓ cup grated Parmesan cheese

Additional grated Parmesan cheese

Cook fettucine in boiling salted water until *al dente* (still slightly firm to the bite). Drain, toss with oil, and keep warm.

Meanwhile, melt butter in a wide frying pan over low heat. (Avoid browning butter!) Whisk in egg yolk, milk and cream quickly. Then add Gorgonzola and pepper to taste. Cook over medium heat, stirring often, for 1 to 2 minutes or until cheese melts and sauce is hot. Remove from heat and stir in Parmesan cheese and fettucine, tossing to combine. Serve immediately with additional grated cheese.

Makes 4 servings

Like Gorgonzola—the soft, mild blue cheese imported from Italy—fresh fettucine is readily available from most markets and from specialty shops offering Italian products and food. Serve as a first course followed by Beef Medallions in Cognac Mustard (page 117) and herb carrots (page 29) with a hearty bottle of Zinfandel.

Curried Crab & Apple Soup

Melt butter in a heavy 3-quart pan over medium heat. Add apples, onion, and garlic and cook for 3 to 4 minutes until onion is limp. Stir in flour and curry powder; cook for 2 to 3 minutes longer but don't allow mixture to brown.

Slowly stir in chicken stock. Add tomatoes and simmer, uncovered, for 10 to 15 minutes. Blend in sherry and cream; add crab and heat to serving temperature. (Avoid bringing soup to a boil.)

Makes 8 servings

½   cup butter

2   large tart apples, peeled and diced

1   large onion, diced

1   clove garlic, minced

¼   cup all-purpose flour

1   tablespoon curry powder

4   to 5 cups chicken stock

4   tomatoes, peeled, seeded and diced

¼   cup dry sherry

2   cups half-and-half

¾   pound fresh crab

The subtle taste of curry and the unexpected blend of crab and bits of apple make this wonderful soup worthy of the most festive occasion. Try serving it in wide-rimmed soup plates, garnished with a sprig of parsley and a bit of crab. Offer hot crusty French rolls and a glass of Sauvignon Blanc. Most of the soup's preparation may be done in advance— blend in sherry, cream, and crab just before serving.

Family-style Minestrone

2 slices bacon, diced

½ pound lean ground beef

1 large onion, coarsely chopped

1 clove garlic, minced

1 cup sliced celery

1 can (6 oz.) tomato paste

1 beef bouillon cube

5 cups water

2 teaspoons sugar

2 teaspoons salt

½ teaspoon freshly ground pepper

½ teaspoon dried oregano

½ cup vermicelli, broken in pieces

1 bunch spinach (stems removed), chopped

1 medium zucchini, sliced

Grated Parmesan cheese

Cook bacon in a large saucepan over medium-high heat until crisp. Remove with a slotted spoon and set aside.

To the pan, add beef, onion, and garlic; cook over medium-high heat, stirring often, until meat is browned. Drain off and discard fat.

Add celery, tomato paste, bouillon cube, water, sugar, salt, pepper, oregano, and reserved bacon. Bring to a boil, cover, reduce heat, and simmer for about 30 minutes. Add spaghetti and cook for 10 minutes longer. Stir in spinach and zucchini, and simmer for 5 minutes.

Ladle soup into individual soup bowls and garnish tops with a liberal sprinkling of grated cheese. Offer additional cheese separately.

Makes 4 servings

Family-style Minestrone may be made in advance and reheated when served. If soup appears too thick, you can stir in 1 cup beef stock and reheat to serving temperature. Our favorite accompaniment to this hearty soup is Foccacio (page 66). Make one large round and cut in wedges to serve, or try making individual size ones, each about 4 inches in diameter.

Hot & Sour Soup

Soak fungi, mushrooms, and lily buds in hot water for 20 minutes. Drain well; remove and discard stems of fungi and black mushrooms. Cut black fungi into julienne strips but leave black mushrooms and lily buds whole.

Bring chicken stock to a boil in a large pot. Add pork, bamboo shoots, tofu, and presoaked mushrooms and lily buds. Cover and simmer over low heat for 10 minutes.

Combine cornstarch paste, Tabasco, and pepper. Stir into soup and continue cooking until broth reaches a creamy consistency. Remove from heat and stir in soy sauce, oil, and vinegar.

Slowly pour in eggs while stirring continuously in a circle. (The eggs will actually begin to cook as soon as they hit the hot broth.) Serve immediately.

Makes 8 to 10 servings

4	or 5 large dried black fungi
10	small dried black mushrooms
1/4	cup dried tiger lily buds
2 1/2	quarts chicken stock
1/2	cup shredded pork (butt, or country-style rib), uncooked
1/2	cup bamboo shoots
1/2	carton (8 oz.) firm tofu, cut in small cubes
1/4	cup cornstarch mixed with 2 tablespoons water
1	tablespoon Tabasco
1	teaspoon white pepper
3	tablespoons soy sauce
2	tablespoons peanut oil
1/3	cup red rice vinegar
3	lightly beaten eggs

You can vary the amount of "hot" in Hot & Sour Soup by reducing or increasing the amount of white pepper used. Serving suggestions include steamed pork buns and cold beer for a light winter meal.

Warm Goat Cheese Salad

8   small rounds of goat
     cheese (1 oz. each)

     Olive oil

1   cup fresh bread
     crumbs

Dressing

⅓   cup white wine
     vinegar

1½   tablespoons Dijon
     mustard

1   teaspoon salt

½   teaspoon freshly
     ground pepper

½   cup salad oil

½   cup walnut oil

½   cup coarsely
     chopped walnuts

1   head butter lettuce

1   small head curly
     endive

1   bunch watercress

Brush rounds of cheese on both sides with some olive oil. Then roll each round in bread crumbs until coated. Arrange on a plate and chill in the refrigerator for about 1 hour.

Whisk together vinegar, mustard, salt, and pepper. Slowly add salad oil and walnut oil, whisking until well blended after each addition. Add walnuts and set aside.

Preheat oven to 375°.

Tear lettuce, endive, and watercress into bite-size pieces, tossing together until combined. Arrange on individual salad plates.

Transfer rounds of cheese to a cookie sheet and bake for 3 to 5 minutes or until heated through. Center each cheese round on a bed of lettuce. Whisk dressing to blend flavors and spoon over each serving.

Makes 8 servings

For goat cheese enthusiasts, you may want to increase the amount to 1½ or 2 ounces. You may also prefer to substitute any number of greens for those listed above. Try Belgian endive, cut in thin julienne strips, or radicchio, or Romaine spears torn in pieces or left whole. We enjoy Warm Goat Cheese Salad with a nice Chardonnay followed by Beef Medallions in Cognac Mustard (page 117).

Fresh Dungeness Crab

For marinated crab, whisk together olive oil, vegetable oil, vinegar, garlic, parsley, lemon juice, oregano, pepper, and salt until combined. Add pieces of celery. Place crab in a large glass or ceramic (non-metallic) bowl. Pour marinade over, toss well, cover, and refrigerate for 2 to 3 hours.

To serve, lift crab from marinade to drain and pile high on a chilled serving platter. Serve celery sticks alongside.

For crab with mayonnaise, prepare fresh mayonnaise as directed on page 44. Cover and chill, if made in advance.

Arrange crab pieces over a bowl of crushed ice and serve mayonnaise separately for dipping.

Makes 2 to 4 servings

Our fireside crab dinner on pages 106 and 107 suggests a special way to present cracked crab. Both are cracked and cleaned as usual except that we asked our fishmonger to leave the top shells in one piece. Then we reconstructed them, in the anatomical sense, to appear as if whole once again. Chardonnay is our choice for wine.

Marinade

½ *cup olive oil*

½ *cup vegetable oil*

¾ *cup red wine vinegar*

2 *cloves garlic, minced*

½ *cup minced parsley*

¼ *cup fresh lemon juice*

1 *teaspoon dried oregano*

1 *teaspoon freshly ground pepper*

¼ *teaspoon salt*

2 *to 4 stalks celery, cut in 3-inch-long pieces with strings removed*

2 *large Dungeness crabs (2½ lbs. each), cleaned and cracked or prepared as described below*

1 *recipe Mayonnaise (page 44)*

Fish in Parchment with Julienne Vegetables

Parchment paper

2 tablespoons butter

¼ cup celery, cut in very thin julienne strips

¼ cup carrots, cut in very thin julienne strips

½ cup minced green onion (including some tops)

1 cup tart apple, peeled and finely chopped

¼ teaspoon dried tarragon leaves

¼ cup minced parsley

½ cup dry white wine

Salt and freshly ground pepper

4 fish fillets (4 to 6 oz. each), such as snapper, halibut, roughy or other firm-textured fish

2 tablespoons lemon juice

Cut four sheets of parchment, each about 12 inches square. Crease in half and set aside.

Preheat oven to 425°.

Melt butter in a wide frying pan over medium heat. Add celery, carrots, onion, and apple and sauté for 3 to 4 minutes. Stir in tarragon, parsley, wine, and salt and pepper to taste. Increase heat and quickly cook for about 1 minute longer or until liquid evaporates. Remove from heat and set aside.

Open up sheets of parchment and place on flat work surface. Brush parchment with some lemon juice—just be sure not to brush all the way to the edges of the paper. Lay a fish fillet on one half of the parchment. Spoon some vegetable mixture on top. Fold over the other half of parchment so edges align. Then fold all 3 edges over *twice* to completely seal parchment and prevent juices from seeping out during baking. Repeat with remaining fillets.

Transfer fish "packages" to a cookie sheet. Bake in preheated oven for 5 to 10 minutes, depending on thickness of fish.

To serve, place a package on each dinner plate and cut an "X" across the top with a pair of scissors. Peel back each section to expose fish. Or, allow guests to snip open their own packages.

Makes 4 servings

We think it's fun to cut open the parchment packages right at the table. Suggested accompaniments include a flavorful rice and a vegetable purée (page 96) with Chardonnay.

Beef Medallions in Cognac Mustard

Melt butter with some pepper in a wide frying pan over medium heat. While butter melts, combine mustards of your choice and Pickapeppa sauce in a small bowl.

When butter is completely melted, add warmed cognac and ignite, shaking pan until flames die down. (Avoid using an overhead fan when flaming cognac.) Stir in mustard mixture and then add bouillon. Increase heat to medium high and when sauce is hot, add beef fillets. Cook quickly, shaking pan often and turning meat over once, for 3 to 4 minutes per side for rare.

Transfer to a warm serving platter. Spoon some sauce over the meat and garnish platter with parsley sprigs and tomato rose. Offer remaining sauce separately.

Makes 6 servings

What makes this recipe fun is that each time you prepare it, the flavor of the sauce can be different. You choose 3 or 4 different mustards (see suggestions above) for a total of 6 tablespoons. For example, if you enjoy a subtle, mild-tasting sauce, you may want to use Dijon-type mustards. But for a stronger, more intense-flavored sauce, try using Bavarian mustard or robust ones containing mustard seed. Pilaf of Wild Rice (page 123), broccoli purée (page 96) and a California Cabernet make excellent accompaniments. And for dessert, may we suggest Almond Raspberry Torte (page 128)?

⅔ cup butter

Freshly ground pepper

6 tablespoons total various mustards (choose 3 or 4 varieties from: Dijon, white Dijon, Bavarian-style, peppercorn, Herb de Provence, or other wine-grained mustards)

1 tablespoon Pickapeppa sauce (or steak sauce)

¼ cup warm cognac (or brandy)

1 teaspoon beef bouillon dissolved in 2 tablespoons hot water

6 beef fillets, sliced about ½-inch thick

Parsley sprigs

Tomato rose, for garnish

Chinese Beef & Noodles

Marinade

2 teaspoons cornstarch

2 teaspoons soy sauce

1 clove garlic, minced

2 thin slices ginger, minced

1 tablespoon vegetable oil

¾ to 1 pound flank steak

Sauce

1 tablespoon cornstarch

1 tablespoon soy sauce

1 tablespoon Worcestershire

2 tablespoons catsup

1 teaspoon sugar

1 teaspoon curry powder

½ cup water

Combine cornstarch, soy sauce, garlic, ginger, and oil in a small bowl. Trim off any excess fat from flank steak. Cut meat in half with the grain. Then slice meat on the diagonal against the grain into ¼-inch-thick slices. Combine beef and marinade, cover, and refrigerate for 2 to 4 hours.

To make sauce, combine cornstarch, soy sauce, Worcestershire, catsup, sugar, curry powder, and water in a small bowl; set aside.

Bring 3 quarts of water, salt, and 1 tablespoon oil to a full boil in a large pot. Place dried noodles in a colander. Lower the colander into the water, stirring to prevent clumping. Cook noodles for about 1 to 2 minutes or just until water begins to boil again. Remove and rinse under warm water. (Don't let noodles stand for very long.)

Meanwhile, heat 2 tablespoons oil in a wok or frying pan. Place entire mass of noodles in the pan and brown one side over medium heat. Turn noodles over once to brown the other side. Take care to keep noodles intact. Remove to a warm serving platter and cover with foil.

Heat 2 tablespoons oil in cleaned wok or frying pan. Add celery, onion, and green pepper. Stir fry for 1 minute. Add tomatoes and stir fry for 1 minute longer. Remove and set aside. Wipe pan clean.

Heat remaining tablespoon oil in cleaned wok or frying pan over high heat. Add beef and the marinade and stir fry for 2 to 3 minutes until meat is seared brown on the outside but still pink inside. Drain off liquid; then stir in sauce ingredients, scraping bottom of wok to remove particles. Cook until bubbly, then return vegetables and heat through.

Cut warm noodles into wedges and spoon the beef over the top to serve.

Makes 4 to 6 servings

1	package (8 oz.) dried thin Chinese noodles
1	teaspoon salt
6	tablespoons vegetable oil

Vegetables

1	stalk celery, thinly sliced
½	large yellow onion, thinly sliced
½	small green pepper, seeded and thinly sliced
2	tomatoes, peeled and cut in wedges

Most of the steps for preparing Chinese Beef & Noodles may be done in advance— marinating the beef and preparing the vegetables and sauce ingredients. You may want to add some sliced fresh mushrooms, snow peas, water chestnuts, or other ingredients for serving a larger crowd. Serve small cups of Hot & Sour Soup (page 113) followed by this delicious beef with hot steamed rice on the side.

Hearty Oxtail Stew

4   pounds oxtails (2
     tails), cut in pieces

     All-purpose flour

     Salt and pepper

2   tablespoons butter

2   tablespoons vegetable
     oil

2   medium onions,
     sliced

1   clove garlic, minced

½   green pepper, seeded
     and diced

2   cups beef stock

2   carrots, sliced

2   stalks celery, sliced

1   can (2½ lbs.)
     tomatoes, cut up

1   bay leaf

1   teaspoon celery salt

1   tablespoon
     Worcestershire

     Pinch dried thyme

     Water

½   cup barley

¼   cup dry sherry

Trim excess fat from oxtails, if necessary. Combine flour, salt, and pepper in a bag. Dredge meat, a few pieces at a time, in seasoned flour; shake off excess.

Melt butter and oil in a heavy 3-quart Dutch oven over medium heat. Add meat and brown on all sides; remove with a slotted spoon. Add onion, garlic, and green pepper and cook, stirring occasionally, for 3 to 4 minutes.

Pour a little beef stock into pan, scraping bottom with a wooden spoon until deglazed. Add remaining stock, carrots, celery, tomatoes, bay leaf, celery salt, Worcestershire, thyme, and enough water (or additional stock) to cover.

Cover and simmer for about 3 hours, stirring occasionally. Stir in barley, cover, and simmer for about 1 hour more or until meat falls readily from the bone. Check amount of liquid during last hour and add more stock, as needed. Remove meat and vegetables with a slotted spoon; discard bay leaf. Increase heat and cook sauce until reduced to 3 to 4 cups. (At this point, you may cool sauce and refrigerate until cold, skimming off any excess fat.) If desired, remove meat from bones.

Return meat and vegetables to sauce and heat to desired temperature. Stir in sherry and adjust seasoning with salt and pepper.

Makes 4 to 6 servings

Here's a satisfying stew with a delicious, unique flavor. You can make it well in advance and reheat, or freeze up to 1 month. Serve with Petit Sirah.

Roast Goose with Red Currant Cabbage

Remove and discard neck of goose. If making homemade gravy, remove and set aside liver. Place giblets in a medium saucepan along with water, onion, carrot, celery, peppercorns and salt to taste. Bring to a boil, reduce heat, and simmer for 1½ hours or until tender. Cool and remove giblets, discarding vegetables. Chop giblets and set aside.

Meanwhile, remove all excess fat from the goose. (You can render the goose fat to save for other uses, if desired.) Rinse goose and pat dry. Rub inside and out with lemon; then sprinkle cavity with salt.

Preheat oven to 325°. Truss goose and skewer (or sew) opening closed. Place goose, breast-side-up, on a rack in a large roasting pan and cook for 12 to 14 minutes per pound or until thigh meat feels soft. As goose cooks, remove fat with a bulb baster. During the last 30 minutes, combine red currant jelly with lemon juice and brush over goose every 10 minutes to form a glaze on the skin.

Meanwhile, core cabbage and shred; place in a 3-quart casserole. Combine melted butter, vinegar, water, sugar, and salt. Pour over cabbage, stirring to combine. Cover and place in a 325° oven for 1¼ hours, stirring occasionally. Stir in jelly and apples, and return to oven for 10 to 15 minutes longer.

Prepare homemade gravy, if desired, and add giblets. Sauté liver in a small amount of rendered fat (or butter) just until brown. Chop and add to gravy.

Arrange goose on a large serving platter and surround with red cabbage. Offer gravy separately.

Makes 8 servings

Additional accompaniments as pictured on page 127 include sautéed apple slices and Brussels sprouts with mustard seed.

1	*fresh goose (12 lbs.)*
3	*cups water*
1	*medium onion, sliced*
1	*large carrot, chopped*
1	*stalk celery with its leaves*
5	*or 6 peppercorns*
	Salt
1	*or 2 lemons, halved*

Glaze

½	*cup red currant jelly*
2	*tablespoons lemon juice*

Cabbage

1	*medium head red cabbage*
¼	*cup melted butter*
⅓	*cup white wine vinegar*
⅓	*cup water*
1	*tablespoon sugar*
¾	*teaspoon salt*
⅓	*cup red currant jelly*
1	*tart apple, peeled and finely chopped*

Braised Leeks Vinaigrette

Dressing

1   *tablespoon fresh lemon juice*

2   *tablespoons white wine vinegar*

1   *tablespoon Dijon mustard*

1   *egg yolk*

1   *teaspoon salt*

¼   *teaspoon freshly ground pepper*

¾   *cup olive oil*

8   *medium leeks*

1   *to 3 tablespoons butter*

1   *hard-cooked egg, pushed through a sieve*

Whisk together lemon juice, vinegar, mustard, egg yolk, salt, and pepper in a small bowl. Slowly whisk in olive oil until well blended.

Trim root ends and tough green tops from leeks, leaving enough tender green top of each leek to bring a total length of about 4 inches. Rinse under running water to remove any dirt.

Place in a steamer over boiling water, cover, and steam for 1 to 2 minutes, depending on thickness, until tender crisp. Cool and then split each leek in half lengthwise.

Melt 1 tablespoon butter in a wide frying pan over medium heat. Braise each leek, cut-side-down, in butter for about 30 seconds or until lightly browned. Add more butter as needed until all the leeks are browned.

Transfer to a serving platter. Whisk dressing to blend flavors and spoon over leeks. Serve at room temperature, garnished with a sprinkling of hard-cooked egg.

Makes 6 servings

Leeks are available in most areas all year long. In addition to serving them in Winter, try offering Braised Leeks Vinaigrette as a side dish for a summer barbecue or offer three small leeks per serving as a special first course presentation. Pictured on page 127.

Pilaf of Wild Rice

Bring stock to a boil in a saucepan over medium heat. Stir in rice, bay leaf, and the 1 teaspoon salt. Cover, reduce heat, and simmer for 30 to 40 minutes until rice is tender. Remove and drain, discarding bay leaf.

Meanwhile, melt butter in a wide frying pan over medium heat. Add shallots and mushrooms and cook, stirring occasionally, for 5 minutes until soft. Stir in thyme and cooked rice until heated through. Season to taste with salt and pepper. Sprinkle with parsley and toss to serve.

Makes 4 to 6 servings

3	cups chicken stock
¾	cups wild rice, rinsed
1	small bay leaf
1	teaspoon salt
½	cup butter
1	cup (4 oz.) thinly sliced shallots
½	pound mushrooms, sliced
½	teaspoon dried thyme
	Salt and freshly ground pepper
¼	cup minced parsley

Here's one of the most versatile recipes in **Taste the Seasons**. *It compliments many entrées, whether you serve Herb-stuffed Leg of Lamb (page 28), Grilled Pork with Cilantro Butter (page 61), or Beef Fillets Provençal (page 89). This flavorful rice can be prepared in advance. Simply sauté the mushrooms and shallots just before serving, toss with the pre-cooked rice, and reheat to serving temperature.*

Cheese Braid

¼ cup warm water (about 110°)

¼ teaspoon sugar

1 package active dry yeast

¼ cup butter

½ cup warm water

1 tablespoon sugar

1 teaspoon salt

3 lightly beaten eggs

3½ cups all-purpose flour

1½ to 2 cups shredded imported Swiss cheese

Egg wash (1 egg mixed with 2 tablespoons water)

Combine the ¼ cup warm water with the ¼ teaspoon sugar and yeast in a small bowl. Set aside for 5 to 10 minutes. Grease a large bowl with oil.

Meanwhile, melt butter in a small saucepan. Add the ½ cup warm water, the 1 tablespoon sugar, and salt. When butter cools to lukewarm, transfer to a large bowl and stir in eggs and yeast mixture. Add flour slowly, and mix until a sticky dough forms.

Turn dough out onto a floured board and knead for 2 or 3 minutes, adding the remaining flour as needed until a smooth dough forms. Place in the prepared bowl, rotating the dough once to coat all sides with oil. Cover and set aside in a warm place to rise until doubled, about 1½ to 2 hours. (Or, cover and refrigerate overnight; remove and set aside in a warm place until doubled in size.)

Lightly grease a cookie sheet and set aside.

Punch dough down and knead briefly on a floured board. Then roll out into a rectangle measuring 12 by 15 inches. Sprinkle cheese over entire surface of dough; fold up like an envelope. Turn dough a quarter turn and roll out again into a large rectangle.

Cut dough in thirds lengthwise to form three long ropes. Place the three ropes together on prepared baking sheet. Pinch the ends together at one end and tuck them under securely. Braid the ropes together; pinch ends together and tuck under.

Cover and set aside in a warm place to rise for 40 to 60 minutes or until doubled. Preheat oven to 350°.

Brush top of braid with egg wash and bake for 30 to 35 minutes or until golden brown. Remove and set aside for 5 minutes, then slice and serve warm.

Makes 1 loaf

Orange Pecan Bread

Preheat oven to 350°. Grease a 5½ × 9½-inch loaf pan with shortening.

Cut orange in half and squeeze juice into a measuring cup (reserving orange skin). Add enough boiling water to make 1 cup; set aside. Place orange skins in food processor or through a food mill until finely chopped.

Cream butter and sugar together in a large bowl. Add egg and vanilla, stirring to combine. Add orange juice and chopped orange and blend well.

Sift flour with baking soda, baking powder, and salt; then combine with orange mixture just until evenly moist. Fold in dates and pecans. Spoon batter into prepared pan and bake for 50 to 60 minutes or until toothpick inserted near center comes out clean.

Makes 1 loaf

1	medium thin-skinned orange, such as Valencia
	Boiling water
2	tablespoons butter, softened
1	cup sugar
1	lightly beaten egg
1	teaspoon vanilla
2	cups all-purpose flour
1	teaspoon baking soda
1	teaspoon baking powder
½	teaspoon salt
1	cup dates, coarsely chopped
½	cup chopped pecans

You can easily substitute three small loaf pans (5 × 3½-inch) for the large loaf, but reduce the baking time to about 45 minutes if doing so. Orange Pecan Bread is perfect for a late Sunday breakfast or brunch and freezes well up to 3 months.

Clockwise from top: Roasted Goose with Red Currant Cabbage (page 121); warm Braised Leeks Vinaigrette (page 122); elegant New Year's celebration, accessorized with collection of personal items, features chilled champagne and Pancetta-wrapped Oysters (page 108).

Almond Raspberry Torte

½   cup sweet butter,
      softened

1   package (7 oz.)
      almond paste, room
      temperature

¾   cup sugar

3   lightly beaten eggs

1   tablespoon kirsch

¼   teaspoon almond
      extract or amaretto

¼   cup all-purpose flour

½   teaspoon baking
      powder

      Sifted powdered sugar

Sauce

1   package (10 oz.)
      frozen raspberries,
      thawed

1   tablespoon sugar

⅓   cup red currant jelly

1   tablepoon kirsch

Preheat oven to 350°. Heavily grease bottom and sides of an 8-inch springform pan with butter. Dust with flour and set aside.

Beat butter and almond paste together in a large bowl until combined. Add sugar and continue beating until light and fluffy. Add eggs, one at a time, beating well after each addition. Stir in kirsch and almond extract.

Sift flour with baking powder and fold into almond mixture just until flour disappears. Pour batter into prepared pan and bake for 50 to 55 minutes or until knife inserted near center comes out clean. Set aside to cool.

Meanwhile, combine raspberries and their juice, sugar, jelly, and kirsch in a blender or food processor and whirl until puréed. Pour through a strainer to remove seeds. Dust top surface of cake with powdered sugar and remove springform rim. Place on a serving platter.

To serve, cover bottom of each dessert plate with some raspberry purée and place a slice of cake on top, positioned slightly off to one side.

Makes 8 servings

Easy to make and delicious to serve. Both the almond torte and the raspberry sauce may be made in advance and in the food processor. Avoid using a 9-inch springform pan—the torte bakes too thin and becomes dry at the edges. We suggest a Late Harvest Zinfandel as an accompaniment.

Chocolate Espresso Cake

Preheat oven to 350°. Grease bottom and sides of two 9-inch round cake pans with shortening. Insert a 9-inch parchment round (or dust with flour).

Sift flour with cocoa, baking soda, baking powder, and salt into a large bowl. Stir in sugar, eggs, milk, oil, and vanilla until blended. With electric mixer, beat on medium speed for 2 to 3 minutes. Then stir in boiling water until smooth (batter will be thin).

Divide batter evenly between prepared pans. Bake for 30 to 35 minutes or until top springs back and toothpick inserted near center comes out clean. Cool for 10 minutes. Then invert onto rack, peel off parchment, and cool completely.

Place chocolate in top of double boiler over simmering water until melted. Remove and set aside. Cream butter with sugar until smooth; stir in vanilla and cooled chocolate until blended. With electric mixer set on medium, beat frosting while slowly pouring in coffee. Increase speed to high and beat for 1 to 2 minutes until frosting is smooth.

Place bottom layer of cake on serving platter and frost the top. Position top layer and generously frost top and sides of cake with frosting. Garnish as described below, if desired.

Makes 10 servings

1¾	cups all-purpose flour
¾	cup cocoa powder
1½	teaspoons baking soda
1½	teaspoons baking powder
1	teaspoon salt
2	cups sugar
2	lightly beaten eggs
1	cup milk
½	cup vegetable oil
2	teaspoons vanilla
1	cup boiling water

Frosting

2	ounces bittersweet chocolate
½	cup butter, softened
4	cups powdered sugar
2	teaspoons vanilla
⅓	cup espresso (or 2 tablespoons instant mixed with ⅓ cup water)

Shaved chocolate or chocolate curls make attractive finishing touches on this moist, rich cake. Or, try making chocolate leaves (page 40). Arrange a cluster of them near one edge of the cake, then place a fresh flower or two in the center of the cluster.

Coffee Meringue Torte

Meringue

2¼ cups ground blanched almonds

1 cup sugar

4 large egg whites, room temperature

1 teaspoon vanilla

Filling

4 egg yolks, room temperature

⅔ cup sugar

2 tablespoons instant coffee (or espresso) mixed with 2 tablespoons hot water

7 ounces (1¾ cubes) unsalted butter, room temperature

Line two cookie sheets with parchment paper. Trace three 9-inch circles on the parchment (two circles are on one sheet). Preheat oven to 325°.

Place almonds in a blender or food processor and whirl until the consistency of cornmeal is reached. Transfer to a small bowl and stir in ¼ cup of the sugar. Set aside.

Using an electric mixer, beat egg whites on medium speed until soft peaks form. Add vanilla. With motor still running, slowly add remaining ¾ cup sugar, a tablespoon at a time, and continue to beat for 1 minute. Increase speed to high and continue beating until stiff peaks form.

Sprinkle nut-sugar mixture over egg whites and fold together using a rubber spatula, just until incorporated.

Divide meringue in thirds and spread (or pipe) evenly onto the parchment following the tracing of the circles. Smooth meringue to the edges until entire circle areas are covered. Place in preheated oven for 20 to 25 minutes or until meringue is set and lightly browned. Remove from oven and set aside to cool.

Meanwhile, whisk egg yolks in the top of a double boiler until light in color. Add sugar slowly, a tablespoon at a time, until incorporated. Stir in coffee liquid.

Place over gently simmering water and cook, stirring often with a wooden spoon, for about 6 minutes or until thick. Remove from heat and set pan in a large bowl of ice. Continue to stir until mixture becomes cold.

Meanwhile, beat butter using an electric mixer until soft and fluffy. Fold in egg yolk mixture until incorporated; set aside.

Prepare sweetened whipped cream and set aside.

To assemble dessert, turn meringue discs over and carefully peel off parchment. Place one disc on a serving platter. Spread top evenly with half the filling. Place the second meringue disc on top so that the edges align. Spread with remaining filling, and top with a final disc of meringue.

Scoop the sweetened whipped cream into a pastry bag fitted with a No. 7 star tip. Pipe large rosettes of cream around the outside edge of the torte. Garnish with a single candied coffee bean on each rosette (or a sprinkling of toasted almond). Cut in wedges to serve.

Makes 8 to 10 servings

Sweetened whipped cream

Candied coffee beans or ¼ cup coarsely chopped toasted almonds

This rich luscious dessert will bring raves from your guests. Candied coffee beans are available at candy stores and specialty shops.

Bread Pudding & Whiskey Sauce

1   *loaf (1 lb.) sweet French bread (preferably at least 1 day old)*

1   *cup raisins*

½   *cup bourbon*

4   *cups milk*

1½   *cups sugar*

3   *lightly beaten eggs*

4   *tablespoons melted butter*

1   *cup flaked coconut*

2   *cups chopped pecans (or walnuts)*

2   *teaspoons vanilla*

1   *tablespoon ground cinnamon*

1   *teaspoon nutmeg*

Sauce

⅓   *cup reserved bourbon*

½   *cup butter*

1¼   *cups powdered sugar*

1   *egg yolk*

Tear bread including the crusts into bite-size pieces and spread out on a cookie sheet to dry (preferably overnight).

Combine raisins and bourbon in a small bowl, cover and allow to soak at least 4 hours.

Grease a 9 × 13-inch baking dish with softened butter. Remove raisins from bourbon with a slotted spoon (reserve bourbon for sauce).

Place bread in a large bowl. Add milk and sugar, stirring until bread is moist. Blend in eggs and melted butter. Then add raisins, coconut, nuts, vanilla, cinnamon, and nutmeg.

Spoon mixture into prepared pan and bake in 350° oven for 1 hour and 15 minutes or until pudding feels firm when touched and top is nicely browned.

Whisk butter and powdered sugar together in a heavy saucepan over low heat for about 3 minutes until combined. Remove from heat and whisk in egg yolk, stirring often. Allow to cool slightly, then stir in ⅓ cup of the reserved bourbon. Keep warm.

Spoon a small mound of warm pudding into dessert bowls and offer sauce separately.

Makes 8 to 10 servings

Very stale bread is difficult to tear so we've found it easier to tear day-old bread and let it dry up to 2 days longer in a paper bag. Bread pudding freezes well up to 1 month.

Thoughts for Entertaining

Winter can mean cozy fires and candlelight, elegance, excitement, or whimsy . . .

Group toys and teddy bears in the center of your table. Tiny trucks or small dolls can hold placecards. Holiday ornaments such as little rocking horses or miniature Santas, make happy napkin rings.

A soup party that offers a variety of tempting soups will certainly warm everyone after a day on the slopes. Arrange vegetables or other ingredients near each tureen to identify its contents.

Celebrate a composer's birthday. Decorate the table with sheet music and musical instruments, and be sure to play his music during dinner.

You can work wonders with napkins. Fold or roll two different colored ones together. Or tie a napkin with a festive ribbon, braid, or cord, and include a single rose or a sprig of holly for a seasonal touch.

String popcorn with dried red peppers instead of traditional cranberries.

Assemble garlands of bay leaves, eucalyptus, juniper, and pine. Embellish with sprigs of dried Queen Anne's lace.

Select a favorite painting and use it as inspiration for a centerpiece or an entire party.

And don't forget . . . lemons, oranges, limes, and other seasonal fruit can be placed on long bamboo skewers and tucked into flower arrangements for added color and texture.

Recipe Developers

Tina Dreyer	Joan Morris
Dottie Ersted	Barbara Oswald
Joann Holder	Elie Skinner
Annie Kellenberger	Chris Stein
Marie Magrath	Mary Tasto

Recipe Testers

Mary Ancell	Ginger Glockner	Pat Maines	Kate Roach
Veronica Arthur	Mary Gutknecht	Tanya Mayer	Alma Sanguinetti
Gloria Baerncopf	Jeanne Hinckley	Joan McDonald	Fran Santo Domingo
Chris Balzhiser	Shelia Hoar	Joanne Meyer	Coco Schoenwald
Fran Beck	Jean Holzman	Mary Lou Miller	Norma Schutz
Bev Beer	Lee Jay	Judy Moltzen	Pat Smith
Teresa Bourke	Marguerite Johnson	Ann Nyser	Janice Sommer
Barbara Buzza	Eileen Kennedy	Bear O'Brien	B.J. Stephens
Sara Calvelli	Anne King	Sue O'Connor	Beth Sweet
Sue Conway	Dottie King	Adele Personeni	Carol Tinling
Diana Dohrmann	Nancy Kohn	Patty Ralston	Midge Truscott
Sue Ebneter	Helen Kriegsman	Marcia Rehmus	Paula Vail
Esther Eitel	M'Lou Larkin	Jan Reimers	Jeanne Yansouni

Special Friends

Narsai David	Pam McKinstry	Donna Nordin
Diane Glover	Weezie Mott	

   A special thanks to our committee: Jeanne Larkin, whose creativity and style contributed to all aspects of the book, from gathering props for photographs and coordinating design to the development of the manuscript; Chris Stein, whose energy and creative assistance in the planning of photo sessions and the development and editing of recipes was never ending; Carol Williams, whose clear thinking and financial acumen kept our goals in focus, and who crystallized our thoughts and eloquently expressed them in writing; Elie Skinner, whose knowledge of food and willingness to spend hours in the kitchen refining and developing recipes was invaluable; Marj Berlin, for the gracious and organized manner in which she conducted our tester sessions; Betty Naylor, for her commitment and diligent assistance in tester coordination and recipe contribution; Liz Brownell, for her conscientious help in testing, and for her assistance in recipe research; and Jackie Scandalios and Judy Adams, whose enthusiasm, energy, and marketing ideas have started the book on its way. Our thanks to Linda Brandt, Ann Remen-Willis, Nikolay Žurek, Jonathan Peck, Bettina Borer, and Bill Coe for their professional attention to detail and their dedicated pursuit of quality.

Donna Hicks and Tita Kolozsi

INDEX

TASTE the SEASONS
P.O. Box 4152
Menlo Park, CA 94026

Send me _____ copies of TASTE the SEASONS at $18.95 per copy,
plus $2.00 postage and handling.

NAME _____
Please Print
ADDRESS _____

CITY _____ STATE _____ ZIP CODE _____

All proceeds from the sale of the cookbook go to Children's Hospital at Stanford.
California residents add $1.23 for tax (6½%).

MAKE CHECKS PAYABLE TO: **TASTE the SEASONS**

TASTE the SEASONS
P.O. Box 4152
Menlo Park, CA 94026

Send me _____ copies of TASTE the SEASONS at $18.95 per copy,
plus $2.00 postage and handling.

NAME _____
Please Print
ADDRESS _____

CITY _____ STATE _____ ZIP CODE _____

All proceeds from the sale of the cookbook go to Children's Hospital at Stanford.
California residents add $1.23 for tax (6½%).

MAKE CHECKS PAYABLE TO: **TASTE the SEASONS**

TASTE the SEASONS
P.O. Box 4152
Menlo Park, CA 94026

Send me _____ copies of TASTE the SEASONS at $18.95 per copy,
plus $2.00 postage and handling.

NAME _____
Please Print
ADDRESS _____

CITY _____ STATE _____ ZIP CODE _____

All proceeds from the sale of the cookbook go to Children's Hospital at Stanford.
California residents add $1.23 for tax (6½%).

MAKE CHECKS PAYABLE TO: **TASTE the SEASONS**